THE SPANISH ROMANTIC THEATER

John Reyna Tapia

Fort Lewis College

UNIVERSITY
PRESS OF
AMERICA

Copyright © 1980 by

University Press of America, Inc.

P.O. Box 19101, Washington, D.C. 20036

Printed in the United States of America

Library of Congress Cataloging in Publication Data

Tapia, John Reyna.
   The Spanish romantic theater.

   Bibliography: p.
   1. Spanish drama--19th century--History and
criticism. 2. Romanticism--Spain. I. Title.
PQ6113.T3   8 62'.5'09145   80-22115
ISBN 0-8191-1276-3
ISBN 0-8191-1277-1 (pbk.)

Dedication

To my wife, Berta Alicia Velasco Cervantes de Tapia

To Professor Ricardo Benavides L.,
    University of Texas, San Antonio and
Professor Eduardo Godoy G.,
    University of Valparaíso, Chile

Acknowledgments

My sincere thanks to Ellen Cargile
for her invaluable assistance in
the preparation of the manuscript
in its present form.

Table of Contents

Preface

Romanticism was the result of a feeling of discontent with the prevailing Classical point of view. It is not exclusively a literary movement, influencing other cultural aspects. Significant events contributing to this change include the French Revolution, the despotism of Napoleon, the independence of the American nations, wars among the European nations, and a literary oppression dictated by the Classical movement. Although the origins of Romanticism can be found in England and Germany before the 19th century, nevertheless, as a literary movement, it belongs properly to the 19th century, and more specifically to the first 30 years. By 1830 it had reached its zenith.

The Romantic writers gave free reign to both personality and emotions, which were usually melancholy, since their real world always fell short of their expectations. They emphasized the exceptional, picturesque, and imaginative elements of life which often led one into an unreal, fantastic world.

The motives and elements of the Romantic sensibility included the beauty of Medusa, reflecting a distinct-type fatal feminine beauty; a distinct Romantic hero, incarnating an attitude of rebellion against established social and divine order; a tragic and destructive amorous relationship; a specific Romantic heroine, reflecting characteristics of an angel of salvation, and a Fatal Woman destined to destroy her mate; an attitude of egocentricity; a search for an exotic atmosphere in other times and places, preferably the Middle Ages; a searching out of nature as the friend and confidante of the Romantics disappointed with their circumstances; a state of reverie which allowed the Romantic to escape the realities of life.

Spanish Romanticism contained a special characteristic in that it lacked the interior aspects of Romanticism as found in the rest of Europe. This is attributed to the fact that Romanticism arrived late in Spain by approximately 30 years.

The Romantics showed their dissatisfaction with the Classical formula by reacting violently against it and by opposing its rules. It required Victor Hugo, however, to unite and lead them in the direction they sought, with his preface to Cromwell, written in 1827.

The principal Spanish Romantic dramas were written between 1834 and 1844 and included: La conjuración de Venecia, 1834, by Francisco Martínez de la Rosa; Macías, 1834, by Mariano José de Larra; Don Alvaro o La fuerza del sino, 1835, by Angel Saavedra, duque de Rivas; El trovador, 1836, by Antonio García Gutiérrez; Los Amantes de Teruel, 1837, by Juan Eugenio Hartzenbusch; and Don Juan Tenorio, 1844, by José Zorrilla.

Chapter I. THE CONFLICT OF GENRES

A. Romanticism Vs. Classicism

The Spanish playwrights during the period known as the Neoclassical period, immediately preceding the Romantic period, searched for inspirational models from the Classical Theater of the Greeks and Latins through those of the French Neoclassical authors, specifically the theater of Corneille, Racine, Moliere, and the doctrine of Boileau the French theoretician. This led to the prevailing French linguistic-cultural model producing, in effect, a period of pseudoclassicism in as much as the Spanish playwrights imitated the French who in turn imitated the Classical mode of the Greeks and Latins. There are political reasons for this francophilian attitude. The reigning dynasty in Spain was that of the Bourbons who were of French origin.

One of the elements which this Neoclassic theater brought forth is the so-called Unities. There were not many Spaniards in the 18th century who read Greek or Latin, however, much credence was given to Aristotle through the French, specifically Boileau. Aristotle is the author of the most ancient literary theory adopted by the occidental world, even though in fragmentary form. This theory is contained in what he dedicated to poetic drama, which is what the Greeks called theater.

The Poetics of Aristotle concerning poetry or literary creation was badly translated and interpreted worse during that period (for example there is no mention of the Unity of Place). It was erroneously thought that the fundamental theory of Aristotle was the Three Unities and that all Neoclassical theatrical representations were to adhere to them strictly: the Unity of Action, which is the only truly respectable one; the Unity of Place; and the Unity of Time.

Unity of Action is understood to be the principal plot of a work which does not permit

1

diversification or secondary episodes if they are not directly related to the principal one. Their only justification is to better explain the central episode. They cannot exist separately.

The Unity of Time and the Unity of Place are related one with the other. The play should occur from beginning to end in one locale, and run its course within 24 hours. For this reason it appears that the Unity of Place is derived from the Unity of Time. For example, if the act begins in Madrid it cannot terminate in Rome within 24 hours.

Fortunately the Spanish authors of the Golden Age (16th-17th century) either were not very familiar with these Unities, or else disregarded them completely. For this they were vehemently refuted by the Neoclassic proponents. Anthologies of the 18th century omitted such outstanding playwrights of the Golden Age of Spanish literature as Lope de Vega. The dramas of Calderón de la Barca were prohibited from being represented by royal decree because it was said that they corrupted Spanish youth.

The Unity of Action further implies that if the play was a Tragedy or a Drama, they could not be tainted with elements of Comedy. One could either cry or laugh, but not both in the same play. The authors of the Golden Age had interposed the _gracioso_ to provide a jocular vein, even in the most profound plays such as _La vida es sueño_ of Calderón, which contains metaphysical, sociological, philosophical, and religious implications of the highest order. This inclusion was considered a heresy in the Neoclassical Theater.

According to the Neoclassical theory, a play opening in a palace and closing in a cabin tended to destroy the Unity of Place, as would the passage of months and years destroy the Unity of Time.

A play of the 18th century Neoclassical Theater was judged according to how faithfully the author adhered to the Aristotelian precepts of the

2

Unities, as they were understood at that time. Therefore, in order to succeed in the theater, playwrights were obliged to restrict their sense of creativity to these Unities, or risk being ostracized.

For subjugating art to the caprices dictated by political or religious decrees, and the demands of custom or rhetoric, the Spanish drama of the 18th century was considered a failure.

Romanticism was the result of a feeling of discontent with the prevailing neoclassical point of view. This disenchantment was not exclusively a literary battle, inasmuch as it had far-reaching consequences in other fields of human endeavor as manifested by revolts against constituted political authority in Europe and in America. The victory achieved by the literary struggle resulted in the surrender of Classical reason to Romantic sentiment.[1] This allowed the Romantic writers to practice complete freedom in expressing themselves. However, since they were never able to achieve their desired objectives, they exhued a feeling of melancholy and pessimism. Romantic authors describe a fantastic world, stressing the uncommon, the picturesque, and the fanciful aspects of life. The individual placed greater emphasis on the value of his own emotional state of mind than that of social conventions.[2]

It required Victor Hugo, however, to unite and lead them in a common direction by means of his fundamental doctrines contained in the Preface to his play Cromwell of 1827, which were subsequently infused· in Romantic dramas. Hugo stressed the blending of the grotesque and the sublime, and the destruction of the unities of Time, Place, and Action. The Preface is a detailed, lengthy account identifying three stages in the development of the human race corresponding to three classes of poetry: the lyric corresponding to primitive times; the epic corresponding to ancient times; the dramatic corresponding to modern times. It also states that Classic rules were outmoded and not in consonance with the new sensibility of that period, pointing out that Drama, the most recent and comprehensive form of art, concerned itself greatly with the grotesque, whereas Greek Tragedy was primarily <u>epic</u> and belonged to the ancient or <u>Classical</u> world, as distinguished from the modern or <u>Romantic</u> world.[3]

The Romantic drama, however, was self-destructive, eventually being ignored by those who at first eagerly attended these performances. The destruction of the Unities seemed to destroy also all dramatic form, leaving only a great formless mass to which various devices had to be employed to maintain interest.

The theater had produced its dramatic effect through the elements of action and scenography in the manner of the Greek and the 19th century theater. The Romantic drama, on the other hand, made use of realistic scenery wherein the stage settings and the characteristics of the actors were presented with a view toward a true-to-life imitation. Natural sites were chosen as being more in consonance with their inner feelings, their melancholy spirits, their desire for solitude, and their perennial pessimism. So abundant were scenes with ecclesiastical settings, moorish exoticism, cemeteries, rustic isolated areas, thunder and lightning, and somber moods, that it was constantly criticized and satirized.[4]

The origins of Romanticism can be traced to England (Jas. Thomas, <u>The Seasons</u>) and Germany (Sturm and Drang), before the 19th century.[5] As a literary movement, however, it produced its greatest impact during the first 30 years of the 19th century.[6] By 1830 Romanticism had reached its Zenith and thereafter began to decline in interest in most of the countries where once it had been extremely popular. Nevertheless, Romanticism continued to smolder by furnishing the impetus for the subsequent themes of Realism, Symbolism and Naturalism.[7] It was during this period of decline that Romanticism achieved its greatest popularity in Spain.[8]

4

The oppressive situation in Spain during the first half of the 19th century had not been conducive toward the liberal ideas inherent in Romanticism, and as a consequence, many of the subsequent Spanish Romantic authors had been exiled. Conditions for their return were finally made possible by the death of the tyrannical king Fernando VII in 1833, and with their return new ideas appeared giving Spain a somewhat European outlook.

No one Spanish Romantic writer served as a rallying point, as had Hugo, although there were some outstanding representatives: Mariano José de Larra, notable for his articles of literary criticism, published under the name of _Fígaro_; José de Espronceda, the Spanish "Byron," who was a superb poet; José Zorrilla, noteworthy for nationalizing the Romantic movement in Spain; Juan Eugenio Hartzenbusch, and Antonio García Gutiérrez, who were outstanding dramatists.

The foreign sources of Romanticism, although not as important as those peculiar to the Spanish traditions, exercised an appreciable influence on the Romantic movement in Spain. The most outstanding source, after 1830,[9] was that of the French Romantic dramatists. The prevalent neoclassical tragedies were replaced by dramas of loose form, always national in scope, in which imitations of Victor Hugo or Dumas were blended in varying degrees with those of Lope de Vega, Tirso de Molina, Pedro Calderón de la Barca, and others of the Golden Age of Spanish literature.[10]

The Romantic revolution in Spain contained more brilliance than depth, and consisted solely in recalling the national past.[11] Dramatic productions were developed and performed for the simple purpose of achieving popularity and importance in the theater by appealing to the current tastes of the spectators. The Spanish authors of these Romantic works were, in general, of neoclassical formation, and, with the exception of Larra and Espronceda, cannot be considered as true Romantics. It is for this reason, and because of its late arrival, that

Spanish Romanticism lacked the interior psychology, or <u>temple de ánimo</u>, manifested by Romanticism in other parts of Europe.[12] The dates of their performances tend to confirm this observation. The principal Spanish dramas written between 1834 and 1844 included the following:

<u>La conjuración de Vencia</u>, 1834, by Francisco Martínez de la Rosa. The plot is taken from an historical event. The setting is in the Middle Ages in the year 1310. Evident is the theme of the struggle for political freedom. A fatal love leads the hero to his death and the heroine to insanity. Verse and prose are used.

The play, <u>Macías</u>, 1834, by Mariano José de Larra is written entirely in verse. The plot is taken from an historical event which is a part of a Spanish tradition. The setting is in the Middle Ages in the year 1406 and reflects an atmosphere of nationalism. The theme of a fatal love affair appears.

<u>Don Alvaro o La fuerza del sino</u>, 1835, by Angel Saavedra, duque de Rivas. The setting is in the middle of the 18th century. The predominant motive is the fatal and implacable destiny of the hero. Written in verse and prose, it faithfully follows the doctrine of the Romantic drama specified by Victor Hugo.

<u>El trovador</u>, 1836, by Antonio García Gutiérrez. The setting is in the 15th century in Aragón, Spain. An element of social exoticism is provided by a gypsy atmosphere. There is the theme of a fatal love which leads the heroine to commit suicide and the hero to die by command of his brother. A chivalric drama in prose and verse.

<u>Los amantes de Teruel</u>, 1837, by Juan Eugenio Hartzenbusch. This drama reflects the legend of a dubious historical event. The setting is in the Middle Ages in the year 1217. A national atmosphere is blended with an exotic aspect personified by the moorish queen Zulima, whose conduct approximates

that of the Fatal Woman of literature. The theme of a fatal love is prevalent. The two lovers, prevented from enjoying a happy life together, die of broken hearts. Written in verse and prose.

Don Juan Tenorio, 1844, by José Zorrilla. The setting is in the Middle Ages in Sevilla the year of 1545, during the last years of the reign of Charles V. The first four acts occur in one night; the last three acts also occur in one night, but five years later. The new innovation in this donjuanescan drama is the salvation of his soul through the intervention of an innocent maiden. A religious-fantastic drama written in verse.

B. The Romantic Motives

1. The Beauty of Medusa

a. The blending of the horrible, the macabre, and the tenebrous with opposite elements produced a sense of beauty for the Romantics.[13]

b. A distinct type of feminine beauty emerged. Degenerate women such as the prostitute emaciated by vice, or consumed by disease, became appropriate heroines for literary works. Negresses of captivating beauty were other favored personages.[14]

c. The element of beauty was closely related to horror and crime. This in turn produced a literary landscape contaminated with desolate, somber, and savage elements, explaining the Romantic preference for descriptions of cemeteries, ancient ruins and abandoned castles.[15]

d. The "Romantic night" is also a product of this motive.

2. The Romantic Hero

a. <u>Paradise Lost</u> by John Milton originates the <u>rebel</u> of Romanticism in the form of Satan. The Romantic hero reflects a distinct blend of sentiments which will become inherent traits in Romanticism, i.e., pride, melancholy, pain, sadness and death.[16]

b. The Romantic <u>Fatal Man</u> is characterized by an unknown family background, a pale and melancholy countenance reflecting tremendous passion.[17] His destiny was to bring only misfortune and destruction to himself and the women he loved.

c. This Romantic hero assumes a definite stature with Lord Byron's Conrad in <u>The Corsair</u> and acquires vampire-like traits with the publication of his <u>Giaour</u> in 1813.[18]

d.   The Romantic hero can be likened to a "fallen angel," a rebel, in the same sense as was the Devil.[19]

3.   Love

a.   Directly related to the theme of the Romantic hero, love forms the central Romantic theme,[20] and achieves a distinct and powerful force.

b.   Love in the Romantic fashion is fatal in that this relationship implied death and destruction which are inherent and omnipresent in the destiny of the Romantic lovers. The rewards of love were not to be enjoyed on earth but in the hereafter.

c.   Incestuous relationships were justified on the basis of the divine right of natural passion.[21]

4.   The Romantic Heroine

a.   The Woman Angel is the feminine opposite of the Fatal Man. She is a beautiful and innocent, but persecuted maiden, who conveys an aura of the divine, even though misfortune leads her to a fatal destiny. This age-old motive of the persecuted maiden is blended with a sadistic element appearing previously in the novel Clarissa Harlowe by Richardson, written in 1747.

b.   The Fatal Woman of ancient origin, related to witchcraft, became a typical character of the Romantic Agony, acquiring the role of a Satanic personage and the destroyer of her lover.[22] Her extraordinary magnetic and fatal beauty and her insatiable sensuality is the incarnation of Cleopatra.[23]

5.   Transgressions

a.   The divine and mundane laws of matrimony clash sharply with the Romantic's natural

9

instincts causing him not only to deliberately dis-
obey these codes of conduct but also to replace
them with a code fashioned by his basic sensual
urges.[24]

b.   The Romantic was motivated by a desire for an ideal state of complete freedom and the
dissolution of barriers between races and nations.

6.   Egocentricity

a.   "Yoismo" (I-ism) acquired principal
importance in the supremacy of amorous sentiments
and served as a point of departure for Romantic
sensibilities.

b.   A clash was produced between the poetic "Yo" (I) and the world which surrounded the
Romantic, causing him to assume an evasive attitude, and to seek refuge in solitude and suicide.

c.   The zeal for personal glorification
was so predominant in the Romantic writer, that he
constantly envisioned himself as the center of the
universe.

d.   This predominant "Yo" explains the
abundance of confessions, memoirs, and epistles
during this period.

7.   Exoticism

a.   The Romantic's dissatisfaction with
his surroundings forced him to take refuge in actual or imaginative contact with strange people and
lands or with remote times.[25] Evasive action was
made possible by means of two forms of expression:

(1) Spatial exoticism. The Romantic situated the plots for his works in distant countries
and places, such as the Orient, Greece, and Al-
Andaluz.

(2) Temporal exoticism. Unable to conform
to his times, the Romantic searched for plots in

remote and vague periods, such as the Middle Ages, which in turn greatly influenced the Romantic scenery.

8. Nature

    a. The Romantics considered nature as a friend and confidante.[26]

    b. Disappointment with their circumstances caused them to seek out and identify themselves with a state of nature which was in consonance with their sad and melancholy spirits.[27]

9. The State of Reverie

    a. The Romantics immersed themselves in reveries, refusing to view reality clearly and rationally.

    b. No barriers existed between the real and supernatural. The Romantics delighted in mystery, the ineffable, the chimerical, and the fantastic.

10. Religion

    a. Tender love and purity as themes of salvation became identified with religion.

    b. Love became a puritanical relationship, its consummation on earth being prevented by death so that the lovers would achieve the harmonious happiness in the hereafter which was denied them on earth.

11. Erotic Sensibility

    a. The Romantics were the first to treat masochism aesthetically, considering it to be a product of the senses and attempted to live a life created by their imaginations.[28]

    b. The Romantic stressed the sensual gratification of pain and believed that the best

way to express pain was through the senses, which
caused them to attempt to experience all the hor-[29]
rors which their imagination suggested to them.

       c.   Erotic sensibility in its most notor-
ious form was the center of attention[30] as a result
of the writings of Marquis de Sade.

       d.   Narratives by Lord Byron and Walter
Scott, called the "black novel," were especially
influential during this period in that they contained erotic elements such as the Persecuted Maid-
en, the Fatal Man and pacts with Satan.

NOTES

[1] Paul Van Tieghem, El romanticismo en la literatura europea, México, Unión Tipgorafía Editorial Hispano-América, 1958, p. 9.

[2] Ibid., pp. 202-203.

[3] Victor Hugo, Cromwell, (Paris, Nelson Imprimerie, 1827).

[4] Allison E. Peers, A History of the Romantic Movement in Spain, (New York, Hafner Publishing Co., 1964), II, p. 12.

[5] J. García Mercadal, Historia del romanticismo en España, (Spain, Editorial Labor, S.A., 1943), p. 25.

[6] Henri Peyre, Les génerations litteraires, París, Editorial Boivin, 1948.

[7] Jacques Barzun, Classic, Romantic and Modern (New York, Doubleday & Company, Inc., 1961), p. 99.

[8] Germán Bleiberg y Julián Marías, Diccionario de literatura Española, (Madrid, Revista Occidente, 1964), p. 700.

[9] Peers, Op. Cit., I, p. 83.

[10] Ibid., I, pp. 6-12.

[11] Van Tieghem, Op. Cit., pp. 153-154.

[12] Ibid., pp. 201-202.

[13] Mario Praz, La carne, la morte e il diávolo nella letteratura romantica, (Firenze, Sansoni, Editores, 1948), p. 29.

[14] Ibid., p. 45.

[15] Van Tieghem, Op. Cit., p. 210.

[16]Praz, <u>Op. Cit.</u>, pp. 62-63.

[17]Praz, <u>Ibid.</u>, pp. 83-84.

[18]<u>The Works of Byron</u>, (Philadelphia, T.K. & P.G. Collins, 1836), p. 138.

[19]Matthew Gregory Lewis, <u>The Monk</u>, London, 1796.

[20]Van Tieghem, <u>Op. Cit.</u>, p. 217.

[21]Praz, <u>Op. Cit.</u>, p. 113.

[22]Samuel Richardson, <u>Clarissa, or The History of a Young Lady</u>, (New York, Dutton, 1965).

[23]Praz, <u>Op. Cit.</u>, pp. 199-200.

[24]<u>Ibid.</u>, p. 214.

[25]Van Tieghem, <u>Op. Cit.</u>, p. 217.

[26]Nemours H. Clement, <u>Romanticism in France</u>, (New York, L.A.A., 1939), p. 454.

[27]Van Tieghem, <u>Op. Cit.</u>, p. 211.

[28]Irving Babbitt, <u>Rousseau and Romanticism</u>, (The World Publishing Co., 1964), p. 215.

[29]Praz, <u>Op. Cit.</u>, p. 150.

[30]<u>Ibid.</u>, p. 30.

[31]<u>Ibid.</u>, p. xii.

Chapter II. LA CONJURACIÓN DE VENECIA

La conjuración de Venecia, an historical drama by Francisco Martínez de la Rosa (1787-1862) was performed in Spain on the 23rd of April, 1834. Martínez de la Rosa ws known primarily as a statesman and neoclassical writer. Because of his political role, he was banished from Spain. In Paris during his exile, he was exposed to the prevailing Romantic atmosphere which influenced his subsequent dramatic productions. One of his plays with Romantic aspects was performed in Paris as La révolte des Maures sous Phillippe II in 1830. After his return to Spain, it was performed there with the title of Aben Humeya. Its central theme concerns the last days of the moors in Granada. The Romantic influence can be detected in its treatment of violence, the emotional outbursts, and the inclusion of an exotic atmosphere.

The performance of La conjuración de Venecia initiated a series of Romantic plays in Spain, and is considered his best drama. Written during his exile, it was published by Didot in Paris in 1830. Mariano José de Larra "Fígaro," the outstanding Spanish literary critic of the 19th century, praised the author and the drama, stating that the plot was superbly conceived, and that interest was maintained in all the acts by means of simple, true-to-life portrayals.[1]

The time of the play is 1310 and begins in the salon of the palace of the ambassador from Genoa to the court of Venice. This is also the rallying point for the conspirators who arrive in disguises to blend with the revelers celebrating the carnival period.

The extreme precautions taken by the conspirators provides this scene an aura of mystery and achieves a high dramatic effect. They arrive wearing masks and are allowed to enter by a sentry who has orders to kill anyone failing to give the secret signal.

Venice is ruled by an oligarchical government which has suppressed all opposition through a judicial agency known as the Tribunal of the Ten, which has been established to try individuals accused or suspected of committing acts contrary to the interests of the state. The conspirators agree to overthrow the government by rebellious means, the revolt to occur during the last night of the carnival season, two days hence.

One of the conspirators is Rugiero, a courageous young man of unknown family background, whose prominent feature is an air of melancholy. Secretly married to Laura, the daughter of the Senator Juan Morosini, Rugiero goes to meet her at midnight in the Morosini family mausoleum where he inadvertently reveals some of the secret plans for the impending uprising. Unfortunately for him, he is overheard by Pedro Morosini, Laura's uncle, who happens to be the First President of the Tribunal of the Ten. With the help of his henchmen, he has Rugiero seized and imprisoned. Laura faints during the commotion, and when she finally regains consciousness, she is in her room being cared for by her faithful maid, Matilda. Fearing Rugiero's fate, Laura reveals her secret marriage to her father. She informs him that without Rugiero she would prefer death.

Juan Morosini, impressed by his daugher's pleas, questions his brother, Pedro Morosini, concerning the incident. He reproaches Pedro for his sternness in judicial matters, which Juan attributes to the grief which Pedro has experienced as the result of the death of his wife and infant child at the hands of moorish infidels.

Juan Morosini discovers that Rugiero has been taken prisoner by the Tribunal of the Ten and is still alive. Encouraged by this knowledge, Juan sets out to save him.

Forewarned of the conspiracy, the government ruthlessly stifles the revolt. Many of the conspirators are killed; those unable to escape are imprisoned and brought to trial before the Tribunal of Ten. These were either horribly tortured or put to death. This stirring scene portrays the stoical courage of the prisoners undergoing torture and is reminiscent of the torture scene in Fuenteovejuna of Lope de Vega.

When Rugiero is brought before the Tribunal for interrogation, he is recognized by Pedro Morosini as the son he believed had been killed. This discovery causes Pedro to fall in a faint. (5,XII)

Rugiero is being led to the scaffold when Laura enters the judicial chamber. She has lost her sanity as a result of her mental anguish, but on seeing Rugiero falls into his arms. Ruthlessly torn apart, Laura sees the scaffold, and realizing its significance, collapses and dies.

The Romantic's desire to employ exotic elements as a means of escaping into another time and place is clearly displayed in this drama wherein the action takes place in Venice in the year 1310.

Rugiero's character reflects facets of the Romantic Hero when he states that he does not know his family background; and that of the Fatal Man, when he asks why Laura loves him, since that love can only lead to her destruction. (2,III) This sentiment is similar to that of Manfred when he speaks to the witch about his beloved Astarte: "Her faults were mine--her virtues were her own--I loved her, and destroyed her." These characteristics of the generous bandit and a mysterious background will also be noted in Don Alvaro and El trovador.

The majority of the Romantic heroes, for example Lord Byron's, sought the maximum of personal freedom and were willing to sacrifice their lives to achieve this purpose, even though they were normally melancholy, pessimistic, and passive by nature. When Rugiero suggests that the uprising may be aborted, Dauro, another conspirator, admonishes him for his incessant pessimism. (1,III)

The Fatal Man was destined to bring only misfortune on the woman he loved, since he was a product of misfortune; nevertheless, Rugiero exhibits outstanding traits of virtue, integrity and loyalty, as attested to by Laura. (3,II) Rossi, whose life Rugiero had saved, shares this opinion with Laura and calls Rugiero a good condottiero. (5,II)

Rugiero's failure in the brief revolt is reminiscent of the fate suffered by Satan when he rebelled against an established order.

Laura's sad plight approximates the theme of the Persecuted Maiden, inasmuch as society and her family are opposed to her marrying a person of Rugiero's apparent low social status. Innocent of her passionate feelings, she is willing to sacrifice all that her family cherishes and her life for the welfare of her husband. (2,II)

Laura appears in a scene which delighted the Romantics, wherein the two lovers meet in the mausoleum of the Morosini family. It is midnight, she is dressed in white, her hair loosened and she is carrying a dim light in her hand. This somber aura produces in her a feeling of fear and impending death, but the overpowering strength of her love and devotion prevents her from leaving that dreadful place until her husband has arrived. Her monologue and the premonition of impending doom is closely related to the classic form of the Tragedy. Then when Rugiero is slightly delayed, she immediately thinks of the worst possible reason for his delay. (2,II)

Laura begins to worry about displeasing her father when he discovers her secret marriage. In her anguish she cries out to her dead mother and wonders what her mother would have done under similar circumstances. The blending of love and death in this scene has a strong Romantic flavor. The lovers beg only for freedom to bask in the light of their love. By contrast, however, they meet in a somber and gloomy site. Premonitions of death and

an aura of impending disaster pervades the still-
ness when Laura enters the mausoleum. Rugiero attempts to calm the emotionally upset Laura and
urges her to enter the vault where they will not be
overheard. She refuses to enter stating that it
contains the remains of two unfortunate lovers who
died on the day of their wedding. In this sepul-
chral atmosphere, an antithetical note is struck
when Rugiero refers to Laura as an Angel sent to
him from heaven to make his life bearable. (2,III)

A deeply stirring effect is achieved by means
of the couple's monologue which is overheard by
government spies; the discovery of the conspiracy;
and the seeming impossibility of having a happy
ending. The Romantic's preference for antithetical
situations is quite evident in this scene where the
arm of an oligarchical government deprives Rugiero
of his personal liberty while he is holding his beloved in his arms exchanging words of endearment
and life in a somber tomb of the dead.

Similar scenes are noted in Hernani (4,II), of
Victor Hugo, and Romeo and Juliet (5) of William
Shakespeare.

The Third Act unfolds in a stage setting completely different from the others and pertains more
to the Classic Theater. The setting is a drawing
room in the Morosini palace.

The sublime quality of Laura's love and her
attitude of self-sacrifice persists with unswerving
loyalty and determination throughout her suffering.
(3,I)

The portrayal of Juan Morosini is vastly different from that of other fathers of heroines in
Romantic dramas. The fathers of Leonor and Isabela,
for example, do not consider the happiness of their
daughters as important as their honor and dignity.
Juan Morosini, on the contrary, is of gentle and
understanding disposition whose only seeming interest is to ensure the happiness of his daughter, in
spite of the fact that she demonstrated a lack of

filial obedience as expected by the social conventions of the period.

Juan is also the antithesis of his brother Pedro, the dreaded President of the Tribunal of the Ten. Pedro, completely devoted to the performance of his duties, follows only the dictates of a judicial code, and shows a complete lack of pity. Juan attributes this to the loss of his wife and infant child. (3,III)

Pedro Morosini's portrayal is surprising for its contrasting facets. Portraying an implacable, righteous man, he nevertheless fails to save Rugiero from the scaffold, even after he recognizes him as the son he had thought was dead. This motive of the anagnorisis was common in Greek tragedy, and the Romantics made frequent use of it for dramatic effect. In El trovador, Nuño de Artal recognizes the man he has had beheaded as his brother who had supposedly perished while an infant.

The loose treatment of the historic element is a Romantic peculiarity in Martinéz de la Rosa. The conspiracy, historically speaking, did not occur on the night of the carnival, but on the 15th of June. However, by situating the beginning of the revolt during this time, greater dramatic effect is achieved by the startling contrast between the carnival, with its gay mood, and the rebellion, with its anguish and blood-spilling.

The scenery of the Fifth Act is entirely of Romantic essence. It portrays the chamber of the Tribunal of the Ten. On one wall appears a poster with the word: Justice. At the entrance to the torture chamber there is another sign which reads: Truth. Another sign posted over the door of the room leading to the scaffold reads: Eternity. It is night, an ancient lamp lights the room, on the table in front of the judges is a book, some writing material, an urn to hold the ballots, and an hourglass. (5) Rugiero will be the last of the conspirators to be brought to trial. The torture to which another of the conspirators, Mafie, is subjected, and the heroic manner in which he endures this punishment without confessing, is similar to the torture scene in <u>Fuenteovejuna</u> of Lope de Vega. His answers to the questions of his torturers are stoical and heroic, in contrast to the atmosphere of terror which pervaded the chamber of the merciless tribunal.

When Mafei is asked if he confirms what he had said while under torture, he replied: "What I have said under torture, the hangman will confirm." Asked why he had named some persons and not others, he answered: "Because at that moment your names did not come to my mind." (5,IV)

<u>La conjuración de Venecia</u> is the first and most characteristic of the Spanish Romantic dramas which reflects an abundance of Romantic aspects. The theme of the play has a Medieval and historical background. The characters appear to be resigned to their fates. The sentiments of the personages are exaggerated to such an etent that they appear to be totally devoid of reason. A sepulchral atmosphere is evident. There is an abundance of common and trivial verbiage, which is almost expressionless. The action is developed in a variety of places, an innovation which created a veritable revolution in the theater. The neoclassicists were accustomed to presenting dramas in which the action in three acts was performed in the same room. These different places were: a palace; a family mausoleum; the palace of the family Morosini; the plaza of San Marcos; and the judicial chambers of the Tribunal of the Ten.

Prominent Romantic motives are portrayed, such as the struggle for liberty against a tyrannical government. A curious incestuous relationship exists inasmuch as Laura and Rugiero were first cousins. However, this is not so much a Romantic motive since this was an accepted custom of the period.

NOTES

[1]Mariano, José de Larra, <u>Artículos completos</u>, (Madrid, M. Aguilar, 1944), p. 402-404.

Chapter III. MACÍAS

This drama by Mariano José de Larra takes place in January 1406. A medieval setting of this nature allowed the Romantics to escape into the past to achieve an exotic atmosphere.

Macías, the most important of Larra's dramas, was performed in the Príncipe Theater in Madrid on the 24th of September, 1834, just a few months after the performance of La conjuración de Venecia.

Macías, the legendary figure, had been a Galician troubador whose poetry is contained in the Cancionero de Baena of Juan Alfonso de Baena compiled in the 15th century during the reign of King Juan II. The character of this poet achieved prominence in subsequent literary works incorporating the theme of a man who dies the victim of an unbridled passion and a tragic destiny. Romanticism saw in him the incarnation of the unfortunate lover. Larra incorporated this theme again in his later novel El doncel de Don Enrique (el Doliente). Lope de Vega had also made use of the legendary figure in his Porfiar hasta morir.

The first scene unfolds in the palace of Don Enrique de Villena in the town of Andújar. Elvira, the young daughter of Nuño Hernández, a well-to-do peasant, has been given in marriage to Fernán Pérez de Vadillo, a nobleman and squire to Don Enrique. She, however, is in love with Macías, a Galician troubador known for his outstanding qualities. Macías had been granted a period of one year in which to win fame and fortune, and as a test of their love, as a condition for the hand of Elvira. Elvira's love for Macías has persisted, but during this period, Fernán has contrived to gain her hand in marriage and has enlisted the aid of Don Enrique to achieve this purpose.

This situation, however, has placed Elvira's father in a very precarious position, and not wishing to gain the enmity of the powerful Don Enrique, has consented to give her hand in marriage to

Fernán, provided Macías fails to return at the appointed time.

A vicious and false rumor has caused Elvira to believe that Macías has married someone else, and since he has failed to return at the time agreed upon, she assumes that he no longer loves her. As a consequence, she resolves to accept Fernán as her husband, and the wedding which follows takes place in the chapel of the palace with the Master of Calatrava serving as the sponsor.

Macías' absence has been caused by the underhanded work of Don Enrique, who despises Macías for refusing to support his petition for divorce from his wife. Macías has returned to alleviate any further suffering by Elvira, knowing full well that he risks his reputation by returning against the wishes of his commander, the Master of Calatrava, who is Don Enrique. His love for Elvira proves stronger than his personal well-being, and he now returns to Andújar to claim the promised hand of Elvira. Don Enrique's delaying tactics, however, have served their purpose, and he arrives too late to prevent the marriage between Elvira and Fernán. Furious, he challenges Fernán to a duel. Before the duel takes place, Macías confronts Elvira in her new home. This confrontation causes Elvira great emotional strife. When Macías begs her to flee with him, her emotions tell her to go with him, but her sense of duty to her new husband prevents her. Completely frustrated, Macías draws his sword and only her desperate pleading causes him to surrender the sword to her. At this moment, Don Enrique and Fernán arrive, arrest Macías and have him thrown into jail to await the day of the duel.

Elvira confesses her love for Macías and begs her husband to allow her to enter a convent. The wronged husband decides to avenge his honor by killing Macías in his cell. Elvira goes to the prison where Macías is held to help his escape, knowing that if they are apprehended, they will both suffer a harsh punishment. Fernán and accomplices arrive, and in the ensuing struggle, Macías is mortally wounded. Upon seeing this, Elvira uses his dagger to put an end to her life.

This drama is the second in a series of Romantic dramas performed in Spain. Still prevalent, however, are elements which are closely related to the Neoclassic Theater. This is especially noted in the attempt to conserve the unities of Time and Place, which produce certain improbabilities; in the exclusive use of verse; and in placing emphasis on the dramatical aspects of the personages rather than on the colorful aspects of the era.[1] Nevertheless, it does represent an important transition from Neoclassicism to Romanticism.

The drama contains an aspect of rebellion against a social convention which forces a young girl to marry a person who is the choice of her parents and not of her heart. Such a love could only end in tragic consequences.[2]

This love passes through three critical stages. First there is the broken promise by Elvira who had promised to await Macías' return. Secondly, Macías reacts violently, not only because of her marriage to Fernán, but also because he feels that his honor has been tainted. Thirdly, Macías' attempt to abduct Elvira after her marriage was an act contrary to social conventions.

Elvira's spontaneous decision to marry Fernán was caused by a feeling of rejection and humiliation when Macías failed to return when he had promised he would. The motive of the plazo serves to intensify the action of the drama. Elvira, of course, does not realize that Macías' failure to return was not due to a voluntary act on his part. Fernán took advantage of her temporary vacillation to gain her hand in marriage. Feeling that her pride had been irreparably damaged, the distraught Elvira begs her father to allow the marriage to Fernán to take place as quickly as possible. Romantic dramas abound in the use of "Oh's and Ah's," and other interjections, exclamations and interrogations, which are voiced by the emotionally upset

Elvira, as a means of revealing the passionate soul of the Romantic personage. This tends to condense the dialogue into words with very little intellectual connotations, and of scant semantic power. Words become the conductors of spontaneity, of flashes, which explode in the spectators ears. (I, IV)

The scene in which Macías proposes running away together as the only solution to their predicament, presents a veritable catalogue of the enamored Romantic's attitude whose reason gives way to frenzy when prevented from achieving his desired goal. He entreats his beloved tó flee with him in search of a place where they can live together, such as "a refuge," "in the forests," "a cave," to break with social conventions, "Break...those... ties," in his belief that only lovers should marry, even if only in the eyes of God in a universal chapel. (3,IV)

It is interesting to note the change which has occurred in Macías' philosophical and sanctimonious outlook concerning matrimony now that this matter concerns him directly. Earlier he had angered Don Enrique when he refused to support his suit for divorce from his wife, Doña María Albornoz. (2,IV) Macías had based his refusal on the belief that God had sanctified their marriage and that no earthly power existed which could annul a marriage contracted before God. His earlier belief runs counter to his present proposal that Elvira desert the man whom she married before God and flee with him into an adulterous relationship.

This situation is encountered in a number of Romantic works, such as <u>Don Alvaro</u>, <u>Don Juan Tenerio</u>, and others. Some authors, Byron and Espronceda, for example, not only portrayed this aspect in their literary characters but also maintained similar personal relationships. Macías expresses his contempt for society and embraces a universal God which is exemplified by nature as the only remaining refuge for an impossible earthly love, thereby aspiring to achieve a perfect union in the hereafter.

The Romantic spirit was known to suffer sudden and frequent changes as it passed through the spectrum of emotions. Macías refuses to believe that Elvira has actually made a personal sacrifice by her marriage or that she still loves him in spite of her marriage. He flies into a rage when she asks that he accept her status. (3,IV)

His passionate and impetuous temper precludes any possible rational solution, and he further comlicates their situation by attempting to kidnap Elvira, and by his infraction of the code of honor with respect to dueling when he fails to wait for the date agreed upon for the engagement.

From this situation, the drama moves rapidly toward its conclusion. Fernán, learning of Macías' conduct considers this an affront to his honor, Elvira provides further insult to Fernán's honor by not only rejecting him but preferring death to him. This so infuriates Fernán that he decides to murder Macías in his cell.

Elvira's efforts against great risks to save Macías or to die with him provide a double antithesis concerning life and death and love and vengeance. Macías is murdered and Elvira commits suicide. In dying together, they have triumphed, from the Romantic point of view, over the existing social structure which had attempted to separate them.

In opposing Don Enrique's plans for divorce, Macías had demonstrated his rebellious attitude. This act caused that powerful nobleman to despise him and to order him into the most arduous and dangerous battles with the expectation that he would eventually be killed, for Don Enrique had no intention of allowing him to return to Andújar. By returning to Andújar, Macías has violated the orders of the Marquis which are serious enough in themselves. Macías arrives while the marriage is taking place in the palace. The seriousness of his predicament can be understood by means of his conversation with Don Enrique. He is trapped between his obligation to Elvira's love and his obligation of duty to Don Enrique. (2,XI)

Further acts of rebellion are quite evident. When he is ordered to return to his military post by Don Enrique he answers that he will not leave without Elvira and that no power on earth can separate them. (2,XI) His disprespect for Don Enrique, who is also the Master of Calatrava, a lofty position, reflects the complete disregard he has for social status, once telling him to keep his mouth shut or to back his words with his sword. (3,VI)

This rebelliousness in the young troubador has a Satanic trait typical of the Romantic hero. It is the same type rebelliousness incarnate in Rugiero struggling against oppression, or Don Juan struggling against God and man, or Manrique, or even Marsilla.

If to this trait is added his passionate and fatal love, which carries them to their deaths, it can be seen that Larra has succeeded in portraying the Romantic hero better than did Martínez de la Rosa, although it is not as extensively developed as in the dramas which will follow.

Elvira's portrayal conforms to a certain extent to the typical persecuted maiden, a theme which is frequently found not only in Romantic dramas, but also in novels of terror of the 18th century. She is the victim of a false rumor, of paternal pressure to marry someone she does not love. Her father is not concerned with her well-being and happiness, but only to gain the favor of the powerful nobleman, Don Enrique. She is also the victim of her husband's vengeance and of her implacable destiny. Elvira continues to display a sense of honor and a faithful role of a married woman as exemplified by her refusal to run away with Macías. (3,IV)

Because of the Romantic custom of employing antitheses as a dramatic element, it was necessary

28

to oppose Macías' virtues of kindness and generosity with a rival who encompassed qualities which were morally corrupt and who expressed profound repugnance for him from the beginning. (1,I)

This Romantic practice of categorizing the personages into two sides, the good on one side who are given angelic attributes, and the bad on the other who incarnate demoniac traits, is consistent with the Romantic's fondness for the antithetical situation. This practice will be so well established in subsequent writers that when the Realistic novel appears it will be very distinguishable. An example is Père Goriot by Honoré de Balzac wherein the antithesis is exemplified by the father and the daughters.

The characterization of Fernán Pérez Vadillo appeared again in El doncel de Don Enrique (el Doliente), an historical novel by Larra. The attitude assumed by Fernán in Macías evokes a feeling of aversion. He has forced Elvira and her father to submit to his wishes by use of a vicious subterfuge and the exertion of his powerful position. He is aware of the love which Elvira and Macías bear for each other, but he insists on her marriage to him. He refuses to allow Elvira to enter a convent simply to avenge himself, and does not kill her because that would be considered as a victory of her love for Macías. (3,X)

The character of Rodrigo de Azagra in Los amantes de Teruel is vastly different from that of Fernán. Even though Rodrigo initially appears as a cruel despot, nevertheless, his love for Isabel is real and noble, and he is determined to respect her wishes concerning their marriage state.

Elvira's father also reflects characteristics different from those of other fathers of Romantic heroines. Nuño Hernández is willing to surrender his daughter for a despicable reason, the favor of Don Enrique de Villena, who supports Fernán's suit for the hand of Elvira.

The drama revolves around these four principal personages. There is apparently no intention on the part of the author to reflect local color of the era.

Don Enrique appears as a secondary figure. In subsequent works, Don Enrique's characterization is effectively portrayed only in Larra's historical novel. This is attributed to the persistent influence of the neoclassical tradition still inherent in this specific role.

Macías reflects some outstanding traits of character. He is courageous, a' gentleman always ready to uphold the honor of women, victorious in tournaments, and a gentle troubador. His unknown family background corresponds to that of the Romantic hero and causes Nuño Hernández to question his status as a worthy husband for Elvira. (1,IV)

NOTES

[1] José R. Lomba y Pedraja, _Cuatro estudios en torno a Larra_, (Madrid, 1936), pp. 369-370.

[2] _Ibid_., p. 372.

Chapter IV. DON ALVARO, O LA FUERZA DEL SINO

Don Alvaro was performed on March 22, 1935, in the famous Príncipe Theater in Madrid, Spain. Angel de Saavedra, duque de Rivas, the author, had previously employed heroic events of the Middle Ages as the basis for his plots. These, however, were written in the prevailing neoclassical vein. With Don Alvaro he adopts the Romantic mode and achieves outstanding success. For the first time in the history of the Spanish Romantic Theater, the principles proposed by Victor Hugo in his famous Préface to his play Cromwell, were deliberately applied to a dramatic presentation.[1]

The setting of the first scene is in Seville. In the refreshment stand of Uncle Paco, the gypsy girl, Preciosilla, and a few inhabitants of the city, are drinking the delicious and fresh water of Tomares. The arrival of a clergyman enlivens the conversation, and when the topic turned to that of bullfighting, they are reminded of the mysterious person of Don Alvaro, considered the finest bullfighter in all of Spain.

Don Alvaro, who had accumulated enormous wealth in the New World, had returned to Spain, and had promptly fallen passionately in love with Leonor, the daughter of the Marquis of Calatrava. The Marquis, distrusting Don Alvaro's motives, had secluded Leonor in his hacienda. Most of the townspeople were in sympathy with the young gallant, and hoped that he would dare to abduct Leonor if her father continued to object to their relationship.

The clergyman, on the other hand, is partial to the Marquis, and states that the Marquis is justified in the action which he has taken, since he knows nothing about Don Alvaro, who could harbor malevolent intentions.

Preciosilla states that she has read Don Alvaro's palm and that the lines of his hand foretold a tragic fate. She also mentioned that her mother had witnessed Leonor's birth, and that now whenever she recalls Leonor, or when someone mentions her name, her mother's eyes fill with tears.

As a matter of fact, having been rejected by the family of Leonor, Don Alvaro and Leonor have decided to run away that very night.

At the hacienda, Leonor has bid her father goodnight. Then with Curra, her servant, she awaits anxiously for their plans to develop. Don Alvaro arrives, and after a period of hesitation on the part of Leonor, they are on the verge of leaving, when they are discovered by the father. In an act of utter humility, and to display his good intentions, Don Alvaro falls to his knees and asks for pardon. As he does this he casts aside a pistol which he had drawn to keep the servants from seizing him. Unfortunately as the pistol strikes the floor, it accidentally discharges and mortally wounds the Marquis. Before dying he curses Leonor, who flees with Don Alvaro.

A year has passed since this tragic incident. Leonor, who has remained separated from Don Alvaro, lives tormented and fearful. Her two brothers, Don Carlos and Don Alfonso, have been searching for the two lovers to exact vengeance for blemishing their family honor, and for the death of the father. They believe that the two are living together.

Leonor has arrived at the Monastery of the Angels which is located in an isolated area and situated at the edge of a cliff. She speaks to Father Guardián and asks permission to live in an hermitage nearby so that she might devote the remainder of her life doing penance.

Don Alvaro, who had thought that Leonor had died, joined the Italian army to fight the Germans. He has achieved fame for his valor, although his deeds of gallantry have been motivated by a desire to end his life, a solution to this tragic predicament denied him by an implacable fate. One day he saves the life of a fellow officer who is being attacked by gamblers bent on cheating him. They become fast friends, but give each other assumed names. Later this same officer, who is actually Don Carlos, saves Don Alvaro when he is wounded in combat. He cares for him during his convalescence and inadvertently discovers his true identity. When Don Alvaro has completely recovered, Don Carlos discloses his true identity and challenges Don Alvaro to a duel.

Don Alvaro, learning from Don Carlos that Leonor is still alive, attempts to avoid dueling with him by explaining the actual circumstances concerning the unfortunate death of his father. Don Carlos, however, blinded by a desire for vengeance, threatens to kill Leonor after he has killed Don Alvaro. Don Alvaro incensed by the threat to do Leonor bodily harm, kills Don Carlos.

King Charles of Naples, who had been concerned with the large number of deaths from dueling, had forbidden this practice on pain of death. Consequently, Don Alvaro is arrested and imprisoned to await the judgment of a court-martial. While he is in prison, the Germans attack and he is freed to join in the defense of the town. He does so because he is determined to die in battle or to retire for the rest of his life in isolation.

Four years have passed; Don Alvaro has dedicated his life to a religious order in the Monastery of the Angels. He is known there as Brother Rafael, and although he has lived an exemplary life, his face still reflects the grief of his unfortunate past.

Don Alfonso has discovered the location of Don Alvaro. He arrives at the monastery and challenges Don Alvaro to a duel. Don Alvaro, on the other hand, attempts to avoid any conflict. When Alfonso insults him, however, they duel and Alfonso is mortally wounded. The duel took place before the hermitage wherein Leonor had taken refuge. Don Alvaro goes there in search of someone who can hear the dying Alfonso's confession, since he does not consider himself worthy of this office. Leonor, hearing his voice warns him to leave. Recognizing her voice, Alfonso cries out to her and Leonor rushes to his side. Alfonso, believing that the two lovers have been living together, kills her with his dagger. When Father Guardián and the monks rush out in answer to a signal, Leonor had sounded earlier, they witnessed the crazed Don Alvaro hurling to his death from the cliff.

One of the fundamental innovations of the Romantic drama is the blending of the sublime and the grotesque, as proposed by Victor Hugo. This dramatic device is very evident in <u>Don Alvaro</u>, and succeeds in presenting a picturesque view of the Spanish atmosphere.

The action of the play begins in Seville, in the refreshment stand of Uncle Paco, which is located at the bridge of Triana. It is late evening in July and the inhabitants of Seville are promenading along an avenue in the distance.

In the refreshment stand there is a gypsy, an official, a well-dressed person, other inhabitants of Seville, a clergyman, and Uncle Paco. This provides a picturesque setting of the Spanish people of the time. The action is lively, and the dialogue is witty, and Preciosilla is urged to sing.

This assembly of townspeople reflects down-to-earth picturesque qualities, and a love for action and boldness. They dislike the nobles for being effete snobs living on their pedigrees, even though they might be dying of hunger for lack of money. These townspeople have strong superstitious beliefs, are prone to be fatalistic, and delight in listening to the gossip heard at these refreshment stands.

The second act also begins in a popular setting, conveying a veritable slice of Spanish life. This is the kitchen of an inn in the village of Hornachuelos. The innkeeper's wife is on her knees cooking. Great attention has been given to portray the details of routine daily activities. There is a student singing and playing a guitar. A muleteer prepares food for his mules in one corner. There are villagers dancing <u>seguidillas</u> as another muleteer shouts encouragement.

For the first time in the Spanish Romantic Theater, common terminology is used. There are expressions such as "a codfish which tastes heavenly," "tomato," "rice," "soup," and other expressions referring to everyday family life. These are down-to-earth expressions which are the antithesis of the lofty language of the Neoclassical Theater. (2,I)

A mysterious person has arrived at the inn and has created a great deal of curiosity, including the gender of this person. The innkeeper's wife said that she saw a radiant face with eyes showing the effects of a great deal of weeping. (2,I)

The last act also occurs in an atmosphere corresponding to the concept of the grotesque. The setting is in the Monastery of the Angels. Brother Melitón, who is reminiscent of the gracioso of the 17th century comedy, distributes soup to the poor seeking alms. There is an old man, a lame beggar, a one-armed man, a woman with a large number of children, and other poor people. This scene portrays a motley assortment of people very similar to those encountered in the picaresque novel.

Leonor's maid, Curra, is an interesting representative of her social class. Her remarks are frank, and her concept of honor, of life in general, the ease with which she adapts herself to changing situations, and her down-to-earth wit, serve to etablish a contrast between the two social classes that each of the young women represent.

Leonor is understandably distressed with the prospect of breaking family ties forever. In her anguish she recalls her mother who could help her during this critical time. Curra, however, offers an excellent example of this contrasting style, the sublime and the grotesque, by stating that God help them if the mother, with her hot temper and high and mighty ways, were alive and knew what was going on. (1,IV)

Don Alvaro is introduced indirectly by means of comments about him made by admiring townspeople concerning his sterling qualities. Preciosilla states that he is the best bullfighter in Spain. This allusion to the courage of Don Alvaro as a bullfighter is almost symbolic in that the bull signifies a destiny which will inevitably gore him to death.[2]

Don Alvaro has had good reasons for not participating in the most recent bullfight since he has been making preparations to run away with Leonor, now that her father has rejected him as a suitor for her hand in marriage. (1,II) He encompasses all the characteristics of the Romantic Hero, or the Fatal Man, who is constantly pursued by misfortune. His family background is a mystery. All that is known about him is that he has returned from the New World with two Negro servants and a vast fortune. (1,IV) This interjection of Negro personages for an exotic effect delighted the Romantics.

In addition to his mysterious family background and his prowess as a bullfighter, he is considered to have such sterling qualities that only an empress would be worthy of becoming his wife.

The third scene of the first act provides Don Alvaro an appropriate somber atmosphere. He is seen wearing a silken cape, a large white hat, boots and spurs, all of which project an air of dignity and melancholy. (1,III) This melancholy feeling caused the Romantics to better appreciate the period of the year when, although nature's vegetation is dying, he is still enjoying the full bloom of youth, albeit mortal, and to delight as a consequence, in a love which is not only unstable but on the verge of expiring.

Don Alvaro is portrayed as a captain in the Italian army, fighting against the Germans. His conduct in combat has gained him glory and fame, and he is known as the <u>flower of the army</u>. This admiration has been gained by his taking risks above the call of duty in his constant quest to end his life, short of suicide, which his religion prevents him from doing. (3,IV)

When Don Alvaro is imprisoned and sentenced to the death penalty for violating the king's ban against dueling, there are signs of unrest and talk of mutiny to prevent this. This scene focuses attention on the magnetic personality exhued by the Romantic Hero who is destined to carry others with him along a path of destruction.

Don Alvaro's dedication to God, as Father Rafael, is as exemplary as had been his dedication to the military profession, demonstrating great kindness toward the poor. Brother Melitón, however, believes that he is the devil in disguise and treats him with diffidence. This belief is further strengthened since he is aware of a recorded incident in the monastery archives which states that the devil did in fact live there for a time disguised as a monk. This tends to establish other Satanic characteristics attributed to Don Alvaro.

Don Alvaro had arrived at the monastery suffering from wounds. From time to time he will strike his forehead and talk to himself as if addressing an unseen person, and his stare strikes terror in the heart of those who look at him.

Melitón's superstitious nature allows him to imagine that Don Alvaro has supernatural qualities. When Don Alfonso asks for Father Rafael, Melitón answered that there were two by that same name. Alfonso stated that he wished to see "the one from hell." Later when the two rush out to duel, Melitón asks where they are going, to which Don Alvaro answers, "to hell." In his frightened state Melitón actually believes that their feet do not touch the ground, and that they leave in their wake an odor

of sulphur. (5,VIII) Don Alvaro himself admits that
he has Satanic traits. (5,IX), (5,XI)

Don Alvaro possesses sterling qualities which
should have assured a happy life; nevertheless, he
is led from one misfortune to another by a tena-
cious and implacable destiny. These misfortunes be-
gin with his decision to abduct Leonor. Forewarned
by the clergyman, the father surprises them and is
killed accidentally. They flee in different direc-
tions, each thinking the other dead. He meets Don
Alvaro and Don Carlos in the course of his search
for death, and kills them both, complicating an innocent killing with deliberate murder. (4,V) The
scene of the last duel takes place near the hermitage where Leonor has taken refuge and here destiny
finally puts an end to all their miseries by ending
their lives. Don Carlos is killed by Don Alvaro,
Leonor is killed by Don Alfonso, and the crazed Don
Alvaro hurls to his death from a cliff. (5,XI) Don
Alvaro, whose religion prevented him from committing suicide, is finally driven by his implacable
and overwhelming destiny to commit this act which
the Catholic church considers a major crime.
Throughout his sorry existence Don Alvaro appeared
to serve as a vehicle of destiny transporting all
the suffering of the world, a victim of mere
chance.[4]

Leonor portrays the Persecuted Maiden of angelic qualities, prevented by her family's social
status from marrying the man she loves. For Don
Alvaro love is akin to religion, and God acquires
the role of a protector and accomplice, as personi-
fied by the priest who was to marry them. (1,VII)
Leonor experiences a weakness of resolution, but
Don Alvaro furnishes her the strength to run away
with him by admonishing her for lifting him to
heaven only to cast him into hell, thereby producing another antithetical situation. (1,VII)

Leonor has undertaken, without vacillation
this time, a resolution to isolate herself from the
outside world. She does not seek refuge at the monastery as a result of an inherent desire to serve

God, but to shun a society which has been very cruel to her. (2,VIII)

Rivas reflects the every-day world, or the grotesque, by means of prose, and by means of verse he produces an image of fantasy and beauty. There is no apparent regard for the unities of Time and Place. The changes of scenery are many and varied, in order to reflect a capricious destiny. The theme of destiny is fundamental, and it is not possible to arrive at an adequate conclusion without considering this theme. Rivas undoubtedly had initially intended to oppose Don Alvaro with a protagonist in the form of destiny. For the sake of cheap dramatics, however, he was compelled to pursue another course of action, consequently, he progressively eroded Don Alvaro's strength of character. In order to create a strong dramatic impression, he had embodied Don Alvaro with outstanding qualities, enshrouded in an aura of mystery, which were directly opposed by an inscrutable Providence. These superhuman traits in Don Alvaro were predicated to provide greater dramatic impact when he is finally driven to his knees.[5] Irrespective of Rivas' attempt to justify the sub-title, La fuerza del sino, at the expense of Providential manipulations,[6] it is impossible to consider one without the other.

NOTES

[1] Allison E. Peers, A History of the Romantic Movement in Spain, (New York, Hafner Publishing Co., 1964), I, p. 236.

[2] Angel Valbuena Prat, Historia del teatro Español, (Barcelona, Editorial, S.A., 1956), p. 481.

[3] Paul Van Tieghem, El romanticismo en la literature europea, (México, Unión Tipografía Editorial Hispano-America, 1958), p. 50.

[4] Valbuena Prat, Op Cit., p. 480.

[5] Allison E. Peers, Angel de Saavedra, Duque de Rivas, (Philadelphia, Revue Hispanic, Número 133, 1923), Vol. 58, p. 392.

[6] Ibid., p. 408.

Chapter V: EL TROVADOR

This drama by Antonio García Gutiérrez, was performed in the famous Princípe Theater of Madrid, Spain, on the first of March 1836, at the request of Espronceda. The play was considered so highly that it achieved instantaneous and prolonged success.[1] For the first time in the history of the Spanish theater, the spectators requested that the author take a bow from the stage. At the time García Gutiérrez was in the Army, but attending the performance without permission from his garrison superiors. To prevent his being discovered, Ventura de la Vega loaned him his cloak to wear over his uniform. The play continued to be performed for sixty consecutive nights, and remains the epitome of the Spanish Romantic theater. It was adapted by the Italian Cammarano for the famous opera of Giuseppe Verdi, Il trovatore, performed in Rome on the 19th of January, 1853.

The action takes place in Aragón in the 15th century. The historical basis is represented by the struggle between the Count of Urgel and Fernando of Antequera. The Count intends to recover the throne of Cataluña and Aragón, which he had renounced at the treaty of Antequera. All the characters of the drama are fictitious.

The young troubador, Manrique, the assumed son of the gypsy Azucena, is passionately in love with Doña Leonor de Sesé, who also is in love with him. The Count of Luna, Nuño de Artal, is also in love with Leonor and is extremely jealous of the troubador. They are also political enemies because the troubador is the follower of Count of Urgel, an enemy of the Count of Luna.

Leonor receives false information that Manrique has been slain, and in despair, decides to enter a convent. She does so to avoid a marriage with the Count Don Nuño, who immediately conspires to have her kidnapped from the convent by sending his servants to accomplish this task. Manrique, also intent on carrying Leonor away, arrives at the

43

convent where he is seen by the Count's servants, who believing him to be a ghost, flee in terror. Manrique without opposition, transports Leonor to the fort of Castellar.

Azucena is taken prisoner by the Count of Luna, who discovers that she is the gypsy who had kidnapped his brother when but a mere infant, and presumably had burned him to death. She had been motivated at the time by a desire to exact vengeance upon the Luna family for having caused the death of her mother by having her burned at the stake for presumably practicing witchcraft. Nuño took added pleasure with the knowledge that she was presumed to be Manrique's mother.

Hearing that Azucena had been taken prisoner, Manrique hastens to rescue her. In so doing, he also is taken prisoner and incarcerated along with his mother. Leonor learns of his fate and in desperation visits the Count and swears to be his bride if he will release Manrique. The Count agrees and allows her to notify Manrique that he has been set free.

Manrique, believing that she has betrayed their love, refuses to leave. He does not know, however, that she had no intention of marrying the Count, and had already taken a deadly poison to assure this, the dose of poison being timed to take effect after Manrique was set free. Only when she falls dead in his arms does he realize this. Furious at having been outwitted, the Count orders that Manrique be taken out of the prison cell and executed immediately. Azucena pleads in vain with the Count to postpone the execution until she tells him a secret. The Count refuses to listen to her, and as the headsman's axe is heard signifying Manrique's death, she screams at the Count that Manrique was his brother. (5,IX)

This declaration discloses that the gypsy who had kidnapped the infant son of the Count of Luna (the elder), had not burned him to death, but had accidentally burned her own child.

The motivating force throughout this drama is a love affair opposed by social convention, which constitutes one of the principal elements of Romantic dramas. There is a powerful rival, a false story of Manrique's death, a religious consecration, an imprisonment, and a self-inflicted poisoning. These are the progressive steps which lead to the inevitable fatal end; the death of the two lovers.

After Leonor hears that Manrique is dead, she enters a convent to avoid the amorous harassment of the Count of Luna. Before taking her vows, she becomes remorseful and realizes that she is taking this step only as the result of her desperate straits, and not from a deep-rooted religious desire to dedicate her life to serving Christ. (2,VI)

The feeling of remorse for this act of sacrilege evokes cries of anguish from Leonor and she begs for divine forgiveness for this affront, and because she cannot forget the passion in her heart which has proven stronger than her virtue. (3,IV)

This religious transgression of preferring the love of a mortal to that of a divine person illustrates the antithesis of divine love versus mortal love. This sacrilege is voluntary on the part of Leonor who believes that God does not possess sufficient power to cause her to forget her mortal love. She thus prefers passion to virtue, along with all the attendant consequences, which is manifested by a sensibility of diabolical origin opposed to a divine love. There is a presentiment of the future when Leonor, escaping with her lover, sees an abyss below her feet. (3,V)

Leonor rejoices in the fort of Castellar with her beloved Manrique, but her conscience is in a constant torment for having committed this sin against the divine being, and she comes to realize that she will never find complete happiness in the arms of a mortal being. This feeling of torment bursts forth from the depth of her soul in a bitter and horrible lament. (4,V)

In spite of this, her love is stronger than her feeling of guilt, and she prefers death to parting from the troubador. (4,VIII) This motive of erotic Romantic transgression is encountered frequently in the dramas of this period, which is here united with the sacred.

Thus she affirms her love for Manrique when she begs him to allow her to accompany him on his dangerous venture to rescue his mother from prison. Leonor's love has proved to be the ruin of them. She has committed the most lamentable sacrilege, and he, for loving her, has experienced nothing but despair and is now on a course which will lead to his death. (5,II)

Leonor offers herself to the Count in exchange for the life of Manrique, but her personal sacrifice is in vain. For once again, and for the last time, destiny has made her the victim of an abject deception. Her hope of saving Manrique vanishes before her eyes. (5,V)

In her last moments of anguish, knowing that she will come before her maker to make amends and that there is no one to whom she can turn to defend her, she laments that she wishes to cry but has no tears from the sadness she feels for having to die as such a young victim of love. (5,VII)

Leonor demonstrates characteristics of the Persecuted Maiden. She has been victimized by the passion which she aroused in the powerful Nuño de Artal. She has no one to come to her aid, even her brother presses her to accept the Count, threatening her with death if she refuses.

The sacrilegious transgression is a very frequent motive in Romantic works and appears to be a form of sadism which was in vogue at the time, lasting until the middle of the 19th century.

Manrique, the protagonist, represents the generous bandit-type hero in the manner of Robin Hood. This Romantic personage was popularized by

Byron, Schiller, Milton, Klopstock, etc., imbuing him with Satanic characteristics.[2]

Manrique's true family background, which is actually of noble lineage, is unknown, even to himself. Known as a brave and gallant gentleman, he, nevertheless, is believed to be the son of a gypsy, and since they are considered to be members of an accursed race, serves as a social obstacle to his aspirations for the hand of Leonor. (1,I)

Manrique feels tormented and humble when he realizes that his supposed low social status prevents him from marrying Leonor. This mystery of family background also surrounds other Romantic heroes, for example, those of Macías and Don Alvaro, and provides them with inherent Satanic characteristics.

The troubador rebels against constituted authority, society in general, and the church. He pursues a course designed by his instincts and refuses to be guided by any human or divine laws.

When he sees Leonor for the first time, a feeling of jealousy surges through him because she is in the company of the Count of Luna, and he has a feeling of doubt about her love for him. Leonor's words, however, tend to reassure him, and he, as do the majority of the Romantic heroes, calls her an angel. This establishes the antithesis, angel versus condemned, for Manrique has been condemned by his destiny.

The pace of the drama is established during the first meeting of the two rivals, who, despising each other, are to engage in a duel for the girl's love. Count de Luna's hatred is compounded by the fact that he cannot duel with Manrique because he is of an inferior social class. (1,V)

This insult by the Count only serves to further inflame the hatred which Manrique feels for him, and it establishes the antithetical situation of love versus vengeance.

After Leonor enters the convent, Manrique des-
pairs, believing that he had lost her. Not understanding the requirements of the order, or of its
religious significance, he believes that she is
held against her will and launches a plan to rescue
her. Arriving at the church he sees Leonor before
the altar and exclaims that she looks more beautiful in sorrow. (2,VIII)

This is the Romantic motive of blending beauty
with sorrow. The sorrowful, the sanguinary, is united with the ideal of beauty. In her sorrow Leonor
appears more beautiful than ever.

At the beginning of the third act the secret
of Manrique is revealed when the gypsy initially
tells him that he is the brother of the Count de
Nuño, then immediately, thinking better of it, she
retracts her statement. This distresses Manrique
because his apparent low status is the only thing
which separates him from Leonor.

The aspect of a sacrilegious love is also developed in this act. Manrique enters Leonor's cell
in the convent and instead of fearing the consequences of his act, he believes that he is saving
her from forced imprisonment. (3,V)

In the sixth scene, which is a scene of love,
there is an allusion to death which establishes the
antithesis of <u>love</u> versus <u>death</u>. Manrique likens
the prevailing silence to a sepulchre, in the tradition of the fatal love of Romanticism.

When Manrique abducts Leonor, he commits a
religious transgression by comparing himself to
God. He places himself on the same level by demonstrating jealousy toward God, and accuses Leonor of
swearing a false oath when she had promised to a-
wait his return. (3,V)

When Manrique and Leonor are at the fort of
Castellar a dream tends to establish the fact that
despite their transgressions the lovers are still
together. The Romantics were able to escape reality

48

through dreams, or even dreams within a dream.

Manrique has been taken prisoner in the attempt to rescue his mother. He is portrayed as the Romantic Fatal Man destined to destroy the person who loves him as Manfred said of Astart. He has committed transgressions against society, the church, and moral principles.[3]

Two aspects are of interest throughout the drama; one is the element of unfortunate love and the other is the element of vengeance, that of the Count of Luna which leads to the death of Leonor, and that of the gypsy which leads to the death of Manrique.[4]

From the point of view of the Romantic sensibility, it is more proper to consider polarities rather than two actions, as for example, the purity of passion and that of vulgar passion. The purity of passion concerns a love which is combined with sacrilegious elements and which originates with the theme of Cain. Vulgar passion is manifested by a desire for vengeance which is related to the motive of anagnorisis, frequently found in Greek dramas.

The element of vengeance is implied at the beginning of the drama with the account of the kidnapping of one of the two sons of the Count de Artal by Azucena, a gypsy whose mother had earlier been burned at the stake by order of the Count because she had supposedly bewitched Nuño, the younger son.

The search for the kidnapped child led to an extinguished bonfire which contained the charred remains of a child's skeleton. The gypsy had disappeared, but it was apparent that she had sought to avenge her mother's death.

The story is enshrouded in an aura of mystery and superstition, alluded to by Ferrando, one of the sevants, who claimed that the gypsy entered his room in the disguise of a vampire. (,I) This atmosphere was extremely delightful to the eyes of the

Romantics.

Azucena, who is to serve as the instrument of vengeance, appears only in the third act. She is in a cabin near a bonfire, singing a sad song, recalling the tragic death of her mother.

Later when Manrique is to be executed the moment for exacting vengeance presents itself, but the gypsy hesitates, for by then she has come to regard Manrique with a mother's love. In this moment of hesitation, between the two contradicting sentiments of love and vengeance, love eventually emerges triumphant, and she attempts to halt the execution by telling the Count her long-kept secret. (5,IX)

The Count's hatred, however, will be appeased only by the death of his despised rival. When the headsman's axe falls, Azucena screams in mortal anguish that Manrique is actually his brother. Then before dying, she addresses her dead mother with the fact that at last she has been avenged. (5,IX)

The theme of the Fatal Man appears to be combined[5] with that of the Fatal beauty throughout the play. To this are added negative elements which increase the sensation of bitter pleasure, constituting the beauty of Medusa. The love between Manrique and Leonor, which should have been pure and chaste, happy, and plausible, appears to be contaminated with misfortune, sadness, sacrilege, and a horrible death. (5,VI)

Leonor's brother, Don Guillén de Sesé, performs a role which is completely anti-heroic, and exhibits characteristics in contrast to those exhibited by Manrique. Proud of his birth, he rejects the Troubador because his family background is of an apparent low status, although he reproaches him for his intention to kidnap Leonor from the convent. He does this, not from a feeling of brotherly love, but to avoid having his sense of honor blemished. This feeling is again evoked when he learns that Leonor is with the Troubador in the fort of

Castellar. (4,I)

In the recurrent Romantic elements found in this drama, there appears to be a great preference for motives related to the Medieval Age, a period which captivated the Romantics for its exotic atmosphere.

The places in which the action develops also delighted the Romantics, as for example in the first act, when Leonor mistook Nuño to be Manrique when they met during a dark and cloudy night. (1,)

The second act occurs in a convent and its surroundings, providing another element very characteristic to Romanticism.

The third act occurs in the somber cabin of the gypsy Azucena, located in the desolate mountains of Vizcaya and reflects the Romantic spirit of solitude.

The long passage in which Manrique recounts his dream, which also serves as a premonition, becomes a vehicle for conveying a Romantic landscape with numerous adjectives reflecting a mood of deep somber melancholy.

NOTES

[1]Mariano José de Larra, Artículos completos, (Madrid, M. Aguilar, 1944), p. 409.

[2]Mario Praz, La carne, la morte e il diávolo nella letteratura romantica, (Firenze, Sansoni, Editor, 1948), pp. 62-63.

[3]Ibid., p. 79.

[4]Larra, Op. Cit., pp. 409-410.

[5]Praz, Op. Cit., p. 33.

Chapter VI: LOS AMANTES DE TERUEL

This drama of Juan Eugenio Hartzenbusch was performed on the 19th of January, 1837. The subject of the play is taken from an ancient legend concerning two lovers who are buried in the town of Teruel, Spain, and which had been developed by Tirso de Molina in a play, also entitled <u>Los amantes de Teruel</u>, of 1635.

The action takes place in the year 1217 in the city of Valencia. Diego Marsilla, who is a prisoner of the moorish sultan, has become the object of the love of the sultan's wife, Zulima. To avenge herself for the sultan's disdainful treatment of her, she has aided Diego in escaping from the prison so that they could escape together. Diego, however, is steadfast in his loyalty to Isabel Segura, his beloved childhood sweetheart.

Diego's lack of wealth had prevented his marrying Isabel until he left on a year's adventure in search of fame and fortune, a period of time which is on the verge of expiring. But, fortune, for the moment, was on his side, for he discovered a plot against the sultan's life and warned him by means of a message written with his own blood. As a reward, the sultan placed him in command of an army composed of Christian prisoners who are to earn their freedom by fighting in the defense of the sultan. In the ensuing battle, Diego and his men defeat the sultan's enemies, enraging the sultana who is their leader.

Meanwhile, in Teruel, Isabel is anxiously waiting for news of Diego's expected return. She is doubly worried because Rodrigo de Azagra has asked for her hand in marriage, a request which her father will grant if Diego fails to return on time. Isabel begs her mother, Doña Margarita to intervene on her behalf and prevent this undesired marriage. The mother hesitates, but finally agrees to speak to Rodrigo, who has some incriminating letters concerning an earlier affair by Margarita with Roger de Lizana. (2,XIII)

The disguised Zulima goes to the Segura home and informs them that Diego has been unfaithful by carrying on an affair with the sultan's wife (Zulima herself), for which he had been killed by the sultan. When Isabel hears this false tale, she attempts to renounce the marriage agreement with Rodrigo, but relents when informed of her mother's predicament. The father, however, insists that the marriage await the expiration of the plazo granted Diego. (2,V)

Diego, by now a rich man for having aided the sultan, arrives at the outskirts of town. There he is set upon by Zulima's henchmen who tie him to a tree and abandon him. They also seriously wound a courier who had been sent in advance to inform the family of his impending arrival. As a consequence, the deadline expires and Isabel and Rodrigo are married. The sadistic Zulima returns to where Diego is tied to the tree and notifies him of the marriage. When Diego's father finally releases him he goes in search of Rodrigo and in the ensuing duel wounds him. Diego then goes to the home of the newlyweds and demands an explanation from Isabel for her apparent betrayal. She dares not tell him the truth for then her mother's secret would be disclosed. When she tells Diego that she does not love him and displays more concern for the wounded Rodrigo, Diego falls dead, the victim of a broken heart.

The principal motive of this play is a true love which is prevented from its full realization by adverse circumstances which prove more powerful than the two principal characters. Isabel portrays the persecuted maiden, an old motive, dear to the Romantics, which was popularized by Richardson during the 18th century in his celebrated novel Clarisa Harlowe. It was, however, so frequently exploited that eventually it came to be regarded in a jocular vein.[1] Isabel makes an heroic self-sacrifice by agreeing to an unwanted marriage. Her father, on the other hand, has only considered the preservation of his honor. (2,II)

After hearing of Diego's death, Isabel's role acquires greater depth of character. To save her mother's honor, she agrees to marry Don Rodrigo. When she learns that Zulima had lied to them about Diego, rather than attempting to avenge herself, she forgives the sultana in a sublime act of Christian charity. She continues to display these same qualities after she is married to Rodrigo when she asks Diego to leave her house. When Diego informs her that he has wounded Rodrigo in a duel, she becomes fearful that Rodrigo will seek vengeance by disclosing her mother's secret affair with Roger, and, in a state of delirium, tells Diego that she despises him. These hateful words cause Diego to die of a broken heart. When asked if Zulima had killed him, Isabel states that it was not the moorish queen who was responsible for Diego's death, but she with her delirious words of hatred. (4,XI) Then she too dies of a broken heart and joins Diego in death.

Zulima displays characteristics inherent in the Fatal Woman of Romantic literature, even though this literary figure was actually the product of the second half of the 19th century.[2] Examples of the Fatal Woman can be traced to Cleopatra who appears to have served as the precursor, leading to the abundant number of this characterization found during the latter part of the 19th century.[3] Zulima sought only physical pleasure, which Diego denied her. In her thirst for vengeance, she sought his destruction. From this situation emerges an antithetical situation of Pagan love as opposed to Christian love. Zulima's love is entirely sensual while that of Isabel is devoid of sensual aspects. (1,I), (1,IV), (3,VIII)

Another Romantic element concerns the love affair of Margarita and Roger de Lizana, which destroyed his sanity and placed Margarita's honor in jeopardy. This association of love with grief and repentance was a popular Romantic theme.[4]

Diego's role has greater relationship to heroes of the Romances, or those in search of the "Holy

Grail," than to the highly emotional Romantic types. Before he can marry Isabel, he must undertake a veritable quest, or crusade, to earn the fame and fortune which will prove his worthiness. When he returns and discovers that Isabel has been married, he does not react in the typical Romantic manner, but simply reminds her that she had promised to wait for him or give herself only to God. (4,VII)

Teresa, Isabel's maid, serves a role much like Curra in Don Alvaro in portraying the difference in social status of the period. Don Rodrigo is sincere for he displays great respect for her purity and sensitive nature after they are married.

NOTES

[1]Mario Praz, <u>La carne, la morte e il diávolo nella letterature romantica</u>, (Firenze, Sansoni, Editore, 1948), p. 98.

[2]<u>Ibid</u>., p. 197.

[3]<u>Ibid</u>., p. 199.

[4]<u>Ibid</u>., p. 144.

Chapter VII. DON JUAN TENORIO

In 1844, José Zorrilla created the most arche-typical, and perhaps the most imperfect, of all the previous literary Don Juans. This is <u>Don Juan Tenorio</u>, which although dependent on 17th century French versions of the legend, corresponds more to the Baroque period than to French Romanticism. Tirso de Molina's <u>Don Juan</u> was a didactic play predicated to the inevitable condemnation of the protagonist. The soul of Zorrilla's <u>Don Juan</u>, however, is saved through the intervention of an innocent maiden, who gambles her own soul in order to win his salvation and prevent his being cast into hell for his infamous conduct. It is ironic, in that, while he occupied his time gambling with the reputations of his women victims, his motto being "me and my senses," it will become necessary for him to die to achieve the ideal love which he failed to find on earth.

Zorrilla sold his play for very little, believing that it was of small pecuniary value. As a consequence, he endured an uncomfortable life, while the person to whom he sold the play became rich. Zorrilla had been convinced that the play was replete with inconsistencies, resulting from his having to finish it within a given time.

The play begins with Don Juan, staying at a tavern, writing a list of all the transgressions which he had committed during the previous year. This includes a catalogue of conquered women and vanquished male opponents. It is a time of preparation for the Lenten season, therefore, the image of Don Juan is contrasted with a very special festival occasion. From the beginning it is uncertain whether he is portraying a lyric or a dramatic character, but as the play progresses, it can be determined that the character is of extreme sentimentality, and that this sentimentality is the only manner in which he can express himself.

The time is 1545. Don Juan has returned to Seville where he is to meet with his friend, Don

Luis Mejía. The year before they had wagered on who could commit the most evil deeds during the year. This catalogue of sins includes seductions, rape, thievery, murder, and duels.

Don Juan is preparing his list of misdeeds as evidence in order to win the wager with Mejía. In this respect two Don Juan-types, two parallel, or double characters, will be portrayed, Don Juan and Luis Mejía. Don Juan describes his adventures in Rome, Naples, and Spain. Wherever he went, he says, "I offended reason, I mocked virtue, and made fun of justice." The women he cast aside and he left a bitter memory wherever he went. Nothing was sacred to him, he fought whomever he pleased, never once considering that he too could also be killed. (Primera, 1, XII)

His friend, Don Luis, has also committed a number of transgressions, but Don Juan has surpassed him. They conclude that Don Luis killed 23 men in duels and seduced 56 women, while Don Juan killed 32 men in duels and seduced 72 women. When Don Luis states that a nun is not included in the lists, Don Juan states that not only will he add a nun to the list, but he will also add the name of a woman who is about to marry his friend (Don Luis). When asked how long he needs to accomplish these seductions, he states six days, although Luis was willing to grant him twenty.

Then follows one of the most famous parts of the play. When Don Luis asks Don Juan how long his affairs with the women lasted, he states, referring to his list, "Divide the days of the year which you see there. One to enamor them, another to conquer them, another to abandon them, two to substitute them, and one to forget them." (Primera, 1,XII)

Then Don Juan tells Don Luis that he intends to take his fiancée, Doña Ana de Pantoja, away from him. This sets into motion a series of devices by the two personages and their servants to foil each other's plans.

This entire conversation has been overheard by two men, Don Diego Tenorio, the father of Don Juan, and Don Gonzalo de Ulloa, the Commander of Calatrava (The Knight Commander of the Order of Calatrava), who is the father of Don Juan's fiancée, Doña Inés de Ulloa. They are utterly horrified with what they have heard, and the profound immorality displayed by the two gallants. Don Gonzalo angrily breaks off the engagement between Don Juan and his daughter, stating that he will never consent to the marriage. Don Juan laughs, and adds a third undertaking to his mischievous adventure by threatening to take Doña Inés by force whenever he wishes. His father's remonstrances are also ineffective, and finally the two angry fathers leave.

As a result of their mutual defensive plans, Don Juan and Don Luis are arrested as they leave the tavern. Then begins a portrayal of how these double Don Juans proceed in their adventures. Don Juan and Don Luis have arranged for each other's arrest. The wager which they had made is so fundamental that everything else becomes secondary in the pursuit of their respective objectives.

Don Luis hurries to his fiancée's home, but while he is enroute there, he is imprisoned by Don Juan's men. Don Juan had escaped a similar situation, and very much in the typical Baroque manner, (hence, el Burlador), gains access to Doña Ana's room by bribing the maid and by impersonating his friend.

Meanwhile, Doña Inés's father has planned for his daughter to enter a convent to prevent her from experiencing the horrors of the world. Don Juan, however, who is extremely agile and ingenious, manages to send a letter to Doña Inés inside a religious book. After Inés reads this letter she falls in love with him. When Don Juan steals into her room she swoons and Don Juan commits another of his transgressions by carrying the unconscious Inés to his house situated beside a river.

An unusual situation which had not been pre-viously portrayed in other Don Juans in such a gen-uine and normal manner occurred at this time. Don Juan, the trickster, the passionate seducer of nu-merous women, falls in love. Doña Inés elicits a feeling in him distinct from that which he had ex-perienced during his fleeting affairs and rash way of life. This causes him to stop momentarily, and in that instant he feels the pangs of love. This feeling of "blind passion" will guide the course followed by his two lives, on earth and in etern-ity. (Primera, 2, IX)

Realizing that the salvation of his soul is dependent upon what is occurring to him, he vows to keep his beloved even if he has to descend into hell to snatch her from the Devil. (Primera, 2,IX)

Thus Don Juan has become the victim of his own denunciations. However, during this magic moment when it is apparent that Don Juan is willing to re-pent, Don Luis, the tricked fiancée, bursts into the room and hurls insults at him. Then the girl's father arrives and Don Juan falls to his knees and begs for the Commander's forgiveness and for the hand of Inés. The Commander calls his act cowardly and hypocritical. Don Juan is very implicit in his declaration to the Commander that Doña Inés is the only means to his salvation. (Primera, 4,IX)

The Commander answers that his salvation does not concern him. The enraged Don Juan then kills both the Commander and Don Luis, who had called him a coward. When Ciutti, Don Juan's servant, warns him of the approach of the police, he escapes.

The first part of the drama is masterfully constructed from the point of view of the reflected tensions and the coherence of the distinct dramatic actions.

The second part occurs in an atmosphere of the supernatural, and although related to the first part, will be impregnated with supernatural ele-ments. There are ghosts, a cemetery, and other horror-inducing scenes. But with respect to the harmony of the play it will reflect the ideal or a classical supernatural aspect.

Don Juan had been absent from Seville for a number of years. When he arrives, he finds that his home has been destroyed to make way for a cemetery. A stonemason informs him that Don Diego Tenorio had willed the estate to the cemetery where all the victims of his son, Don Juan Tenorio, were to be buried.

Don Juan kneels before the tomb of Doña Inés and expresses his grief. It is difficult to determine why Doña Inés had died. She is simply an innocent victim of circumstances, much in the manner of the Romantic Persecuted Maiden. The ghost of Doña Inés appears to Don Juan and informs him that God has allowed her to wait for him to persuade him to repent or else she will be condemned along with him. When she disappears, he believes that it was all an hallucination. However, he notices that the statue of Inés has also disappeared.

At that moment two of Don Juan's former companions make their appearance. It is Centellas and Avellaneda, who, upon seeing him in a frightened state, chide him for his fear of dead people. Don Juan then invites them to dine with him, and to show that he is not afraid of the dead, he also invites the statue of the Commander. (Segunda, 1,VI)

A perfect harmony or equilibrium between the first part and the second part is evident. The first part occurred in the world of reality, now the second part is taking place in the world of the supernatural. The dramatic tension is greatly enhanced, for Don Juan is no longer pitting himself against the human elements but against the supernatural, against divine order, as stated by the those of Doña Inés. (Segunda, 2,IV)

While Don Juan and his two friends are having dinner, the statue of the Commander joins him and Ciutti, and the two friends faint. Don Juan, thinking that he is being made the victim of a joke by his friends, asks the statue of Don Gonzalo to eat. The statue tells him to repent for there is another life after death, and that since Don Juan is to die the following day, he is here to warn him of the consequences. These expostulations by the statue appear to be superfluous because Don Juan is not a free thinker and he is not an atheist. He is merely a libertine and has never doubted the existence of eternity so that the statement of the Commander appears to be unnecessary with respect to the economy of the play. (Segunda, 2,II)

However, two things in this admonishment are pertinent. The statue is being generous in telling Don Juan that he has an entire day to consider his sinful life, and that if he does not repent he will be condemned. This is quite a contrast from the original Don Juan of Tirso de Molina, who continually proclaimed: "There is plenty of time." In an attempt to dispel the possibility that he might be dreaming, Don Juan fires his pistol at the statue, who disappears through the walls. The ghost of Doña Inés again appears and begs that he heed the advice of the statue. Don Juan, however, believes that he has been made the victim of a hoax by his two friends who in turn accuse him of the same offense. A duel ensues and immediately afterwards Don Juan is seen walking to the cemetery regretting having to kill his two friends.

At the cemetery he summons the Commander who had invited him to dine with him there. A table with snakes, bones, and fire appears. All the tombs open except the tomb of Inés. When the statue informs Don Juan that his time has expired, he realizes that it was he who had been killed in the duel. He sees a funeral march by and is informed that it is his funeral. This is reminiscent of El estudiante de Salamanca of Espronceda, where Felix de Montemar witnesses his own funeral and dances with the skeleton of a dead woman.

The statue will again admonish Don Juan by telling him that he still has time to repent and save his soul. Don Juan, however, doubts that in one moment he can blot out thirty years of transgressions. With this the statue tells him that he must join him and extends his hand. Don Juan, believing that the statue does so as a gesture of friendship, clasps his hand, but attempts to withdraw it when the statue tells him that he is taking him to hell.

Don Juan now realizes the seriousness of his predicament, and pleads for the moment still remaining. Calling upon God, he asks that, if it is possible to repent, he so does, that he believes in God and asks his mercy. (Segunda, 3,II) At that moment Doña Inés appears, takes his hand, which he had extended heavenward, and both fall dead. (Segunda, 3,IV)

Zorrilla was acquainted with the personages created by Byron and Espronceda, but his version of Don Juan reflects the Baroque tradition more than it does the Romantic period.

In the first place, Don Juan Tenorio does not portray the distinctive characteristics of the Romantic Hero. His origin is well-known; he does not attempt to conceal his past nor his present activities; he is not involved in a struggle for an ideal love as the only motivating force of his life; he is not melancholy but rather extremely dynamic.

He displays Satanic and rebellious elements of the Romantic personage, which lead him to commit numerous transgressions against the law, society, established customs, and the church.

The first appearance of Don Juan reflects a quarrelsome attitude and a confidence in his ability as a swordsman. His words are not just a display of bravado. While writing his letter in the tavern of Buttareli, he threatens to punish some noisy revelers, and when he leaves the tavern, true to his word, he engages in a scuffle with them.

The adventures of Don Juan, which in Tirso's

play appeared as portrayed action, are conveyed in Zorrilla's by means of narration, since there is a different center of interest. In Tirso's the most important aspects were the sudden changes in the personage in his fooling of women to satisfy his instincts and pride. In Zorrilla's, there is a greater interest in the dramatic aspects. This Don Juan differs from that of Moliere's in that he is not a hypocrite, which is the major defensive characteristic of Don Juan ou Le Festin de Pierre. (Primera, 1,XII)

The abduction of Doña Inés reveals a similar situation in El trovador, in which there is a conscious awareness of committing this religious transgression. In Don Juan, on the other hand, Inés is a pure and innocent person. She swoons in the arms of Don Juan and does not take an active part in the abduction. Afterwards, the truth of the matter is not revealed to her, Don Juan falsely stating that the convent was destroyed by flames and that he had to rescue her from the fire. Furthermore, she had been placed in the convent, not to become a nun, but for the customary period of schooling given girls of her social status. Therefore, this cannot be considered as a religious transgression in the strictest sense of the word.

The title of the Third Act of the First Part, is more a part of Romanticism than any of the previous acts, and is more closely related to the Baroque sensibility; Licentiousness and Scandal and Dexterity. The act entitled Desecration is somewhat similar to scenes of the monasteries on Don Alvaro and El trovador.

The action develops to the point where Don Juan conspires with Brígida, Doña Inés's maid. Don Juan does not consider Inés as just another adventure motivated by his desire to play a trick on his victim, for he has come to the realization that he has fallen in love with her. (Primera, 2,IX)

This situation has thus been reversed. It will not be Don Juan, who, as he says, will snatch this pure and innocent girl from the arms of Satan, but rather, it will be the soul of Doña Inés, struggling against evil, who will save him from damnation. This Satanic allusion attributed to Don Juan is noticeably repetitive.

Don Luis, standing before the house of his sweetheart, whom he wishes to protect from Don Juan's villainy, claims that he has the Devil in him. (Primera, 2,II) Don Gonzalo has the same opinion of him when he admonishes the Mother Superior for not being more watchful over Doña Inés. (Primera, 2,VIII)

The first three acts constitute' the life of Don Juan. He is portrayed as rebellious, quarrelsome, a trickster, courageous, proud, and Satanic.

The Fourth Act, which completes the First Part, is entitled The Devil at the Gates of Heaven, and establishes the critical point in the life of the protagonist. Don Juan falls in love, and believes that this new and marvelous sensation can lead to his redemption. Destiny, however, decides otherwise, and this time the eternal trickster is himself tricked.

There is a continued and persistent attribution of Satanic qualities to Don Juan. Ciutti, for instance, states that he believes that Don Juan is the Devil in human flesh, because only Satan would do the things Don Juan does. (Primera, 4,I) Doña Inés attributes her fascination for him, to a mysterious potion, or magnetic qualities given to him by Satan. Irrespective of this, the seducer has become a slave of his intended victim. (Primera, 4, III)

This spiritual rebirth establishes the difference between Zorrilla's Don Juan and all the others up to this point. This regeneration does not provide happiness in this life, but it assures the salvation of his soul. The love of Doña Inés reveals to him a new and unknown world, a true love which leads to his salvation, that it is not the

Devil but perhaps God who is responsible for this love by way of winning him over. (Primera, 4,III)

The proverbial pride and rebelliousness of the protagonist are revealed in the words he speaks while prostrated at the feet of the Commander, and clearly exhibits his complete conversion. (Primera, 4,IX) His intentions, although beneficent, are tragic and frantic, and are shattered by the obdurate attitude of the Commander who refuses to believe that Don Juan could have undergone such a sudden change. His only desire is to avenge himself for the blemish on his honor. He is not concerned that Don Juan's salvation is in peril. He prefers to have his daughter dead than married to such a vile person.

The Commander dies from a pistol shot, as did the father of Leonor in <u>Don Alvaro</u>. In this instance, however, the Commander was not killed accidentally, but deliberately and brutally murdered in an impatient effort to destroy the person who constituted a formidable obstacle to Don Juan's happiness.

After killing Don Luis and escaping from the police, he again reverts to his former habits as the trickster rebuking Providence for its inflexibility believing that it would be responsible for his future conduct. (Primera, 4,X)

The second part of the drama corresponds to the religious and the fantastic. It represents the death of the protagonist and develops the theme of the invited stone guest. This part concerns the mystery of hopeful anguish. It transpires between shadows and apparitions, and between tombs and moving statues. Don Juan in the first part was characterized as agile, a seducer, a ruffian, and of having the possibility of being redeemed. Fate and a providential justice prevented this. The previous episodes were rapid and intense. Those which follow are slow, melancholy, spectral, and misty.

The last act in the first part was the key to

that part. In the second part the center of intensity is at the beginning. This scene is adequately entitled, The ghost of Doña Inés, the action taking place in a calm summer night and illuminated by an extremely clear moon. Don Juan appears, full of new adventures, but grieving for the past. He uncovers himself respectfully before the tomb of his father. The sculptor, not knowing who he is describes Don Juan as a cruel, sanguinary, and Satanic person, who caused all these deaths. (Seguna, 1,II)

In the characteristic Romantic manner, when alone with his memories, surrounded by this spectral atmosphere, he begins a soliloquy which is so different from other Don Juans. His lament is remorseful and anguished. He laments the many beautiful nights which he foolishly lost in the pursuit of a life of crime. (Segunda, 1,III)

The ghost of Doña Inés then appears and tells him of the celestial arrangement which she has made in the hopes of saving his soul.

The Second Act of the Second Part develops the theme of the invitation to the stone guest, the macabre banquet, which has its origins in the remote past. This invitation has an abundance of antecedents in folklore. An early use of this theme consists of an invitation, in jest, to a skull. The incident concerns an individual who finds a skull lying on the ground; he kicks it and invites it to dine with him. The results of this invitation are rather diverse. In Danish and German folklore, the dead person takes the offender to the other world for two or three centuries, at which time he is returned to earth. In the stories originating in Breton and France, the offender pays with his life. According to an account attributed to Picard, the offender finds himself at a banquet surrounded by joyous phantoms where the festivities and dancing continue until a cock crows. In the Gascon and Portuguese stories, the offender assists in the dinner with the dead man, but is saved from retribution by following the advice of a clergyman, or by wearing garments given him by a priest, or by carrying sacred relics on his person. In these instances he is simply admonished. A Tirelese and Icelandic account states that the wife or fiancée saves the offender from vengeance at the hands of the dead man.

A variation of these stories was dramatized and presented by German Jesuits in the 17th and 18th centuries. It was presented for the first time in Ingolstadt, Germany, in the autumn of 1615, approximately 15 years before the first edition of the drama known as El Burlador de Sevilla, by Tirso de Molina. This drama consisted of a Count Leoncio, who, under the spell of the Machiavellian doctrine, disbelieves in the hereafter. While passing through a cemetery he finds a skull which he kicks in jest, and tells it that if the skull understands him to join him at dinner with other invitees. When Leoncio and his company sit for dinner a skeleton arrives. Efforts to eject him fail. The skeleton tells the frightened participants that he is the grandfather of Leoncio and has come to demonstrate to the Count the immortality of the soul, then takes the Count with him in several pieces.

The sense of horror which the macabre scene in the cemetery is intended to produce, is somewhat attenuated by the presence of Doña Inés and the anticipation of salvation. The final act in which the repentant sinner is saved is entitled, The mercy of God and the apotheosis. Don Juan is no longer the proud person of the past. The fear of God has made him cautious, but as previously mentioned, he doubts the possibility of his salvation. He will witness his own funeral, as did Felix de Montemar in El estudiante de Salamanca, but only Don Juan will achieve salvation, because he has Doña Inés, who has maintained a constant vigil in her tomb in the hope of saving him.

Zorrilla, with rare ability, has placed at the side of Don Juan, a second "Don Juan," who at times appears to be his imitator, at other times, his rival. This is the person of Don Luis Mejía. In the first scene his role is to boast of his adventures which were the consequence of a wager. Even though

70

he is defeated, he is an exemplary personification of scandals and conquests. He is a type of brigand as demonstrated by his assault on the Episcopal Palace of Ghent. This conduct is distinct from those concerning the love affairs and duels of Don Juan. Don Luis, however, is desirous of changing his way of life. He is a love-crazed young man who would have ended his role as a happily married man if Don Juan had not added his fiancée, Doña Ana de Pantoja, to his list of conquests. Instead, he dies at the end of his former friend's sword.

Don Gonzalo de Ulloa, as the father, portrays his role somewhat differently from previous fathers of Romantic heroines. He considers the welfare of his daughter and prudently investigates the truth of the stories concerning Don Juan's conduct. He disguises himself, and, along with the Commander, is witness to the meeting between Don Juan and Don Luis. His sense of fair play prompts him to take this recourse. When he discovers that the stories about Don Juan are correct, he concludes that he would rather see his daughter dead than married to him. (Primera, 1,VI)

Doña Inés is a figure of importance, and, even though her activities on earth were slight, she acquires greater importance in the second part as a spiritual being, since she is the means to Don Juan's salvation. (Primera, 4,III)

The scene in the third act is prodigious in its blending of Doña Inés with Brígida, who corresponds to the character of a "Celestina." The book, the letter, the diverse reactions, all lead toward the budding of an innocent childish love, which blooms with the encouragement and subtle suggestions of the procuress. This prepares the emotional outlook of Doña Inés so that she will become easy prey for the abduction in the following act.

Ciutti, Don Juan's servant, is the most flexible figure. Although he allows himself to admire Don Juan, he does so at a distance. The servant is commonly portrayed as a contrast to his master.

Catalinón in <u>El Burlador</u>, is the most prominent figure next to Don Juan. In Zorrilla, Ciutti remains solely a peripheral figure and is portrayed in a manner that will provoke laughter. He is derived from the traditional <u>gracioso</u>, who at best was gay, witty, and even tragicomical, supplying the realistic or cynical counterpoint which enhanced the theme of the central or major character.

NOTES

[1]Menéndez Pidal, Ramón, <u>Estudios Literarios</u>, (Colección Austral, Espasa-Calpe, S.A., Madrid, 1957), pp. 83-107.

Chapter VIII. BIBLIOGRAPHY

Almagro San Martín, Melchor de, Artículos completos de Larra, Madrid, Aguilar, 1944.

Alonso Cortés, Narciso, Prólogo a Poesías de Zorrilla en Clásicos Castellanos, 63, Madrid, Espasa-Calpe, 1944.

Prólogo a Teatro de Bretón de los Herreros, en Clásicos Castellanos, 92, Madrid, Espasa-Calpe, 1943.

Artz, Frederick B., From the Renaissance to Romanticism, Chicago, University of Chicago Press, 1965.

Babbitt, Irving, Rousseau and Romanticism, Ohio, The World Publishing Co., 1964.

Barzun, Jacques, Classic, Romantic and Modern, New York, Anchor, Doubleday and Co., Inc., 1961.

Beers, Henry A., A History of English Romanticism in the Eighteenth Century, New York, Dover Publications, Inc., 1898.

Boussagol, Gabriel, Angel de Saavedra, duc de Rivas, Toulouse, Imprimerie et librairie Edouard Privat, 1926.

Brandes, George, Revolution and Reaction in the Nineteenth Century French Literature, New York, Russel and Russel.

Castro, Américo, Prólogo a Comedias de Tirso de Molina, 2, Madrid, Espasa-Calpe, 1952.

Chateaubriand, M. Le Vicomte, Atala, René, Les Abencérages, Voyage en Amerique, Paris, Firmin-Didot et Cie. Imprimeurs-Editeurs, 1805.

Disternas, Lelia B., Materia y Manera en el Teatro Romántico Español, Universidad de Chile, 1958.

Clement, Nemours Honore, Romanticism in France New York, L.A.A., 1939.

Collins, T.K. and P.G., The Works of Byron, Philadelphia, 1836.

Cuevas, Juan de la, El infamador, Madrid, Clásicos Castellanos, 60, Espasa-Calpe, 1953.

Diáz-Plaja, Fernando, Antología del romanticismo Español, Madrid, Revista Occidente, 1959.

Diáz-Plaja, Guillermo, Introducción al estudio del romanticismo Español, Madrid, Espasa-Calpe, 1942.

Barroco y Romanticismo en Ensayos elegidos, Revista de Occidente, 1965.

Espronceda, José de, Poesías y El estudiante de Salamanca, Madrid, Clásicos Castellanos, 47, Espasa-Calpe, 1962.

Frye, Prosser Hall, Romance and Tragedy, Lincoln, University of Nebraska Press, 1964.

García Gutiérrez, Antonio, El trovador in El teatro Español of Federico Carlos Sainz de Robles, Tomo VI, M. Aguilar, 1943.

García Mercadal, J., Historia del romanticismo en España, Barcelona Editorial Labor, S.A., 1943.

Gil Albacete, Alvaro, Prólogo al Teatro de Hartzenbusch, in Clásicos Castellanos, 113, Madrid, Espasa-Calpe, 1947.

Green, Otis H., Spain and the Western Tradition, Wisconsin, University of Wisconsin Press, Vol. I, 1964.

Hartzenbusch, Juan Eugenio, Los amantes de Teruel, Buenos Aires, Editorial Sopena, S.R.L., 1950.

          Los amantes de
Teruel, y La jura en Santa Gadea, Clásicos Castellanos, 113, Madrid, Espasa-Calpe, 1947.

  Hauser, Arnold, The Social History of Art,
Vol. 3, New York, Vintage Books, 1958.

  Hugo, Victor, Cromwell, Great Britain, Imprimerie Nelson, Edimbourg, Ecosse, 1827.

        Hernani, París, Edition Ne
Varietur, 1836.

  Kayser, Wolfgang, The Grotesque in Art and
Literature, New York, McGraw-Hill Book Co., 1966.

  Larra, Mariano José de, El doncel de Don Enrique el Doliente, Santiago, Editorial Ercilla,
1936.

  Lomba y Pedraja, José R., Prólogo a Artículos
de Larra, Clásicos Castellanos, 52, and 77, Madrid,
Espasa-Calpe, 1950.

        Prólogo a Teatro de
García Gutiérrez, 65, Clásicos Castellanos, Madrid,
Espasa-Calpe, 1941.

  Lope de Vega, Felix, Fuente Ovejuna and La
dama boba, Dell, 1964.

        Arte neuvo de hacer co-
medias, 842, Buenos Aires, Espasa-Calpe, 1948.

  Lukacs, Georg, The Historical Novel, Boston,
Beacon Press, 1963.

  Maeztu, Ramiro de, Don Quijote, Don Juan, y La
Celestina, Buenos Aires, Espasa-Calpe, 31, 1952.

  Mandel, Oscar, The Theatre of Don Juan, Lincoln, University of Nebraska Press, 1963.

Martínez de la Rosa, Francisco, <u>Obras dramá-</u><u>ticas</u>, 107, Clásicos Castellanos, Madrid, Espasa-Calpe, 1947.

<u>Poética</u>, Paris 1843.

Maugis, Henri, <u>Lamartine, Meditations</u>, Paris, Classiques Larousse, 1934.

Menéndez Pidal, Ramón, <u>Estudios Literarios</u>, Colección Austral, Espasa-Calpe, S.A., Madrid, 1957.

Michaud, Guy-Van Tieghem, Paul, <u>Le romantisme</u>, Paris, Classique Hachette, 1952.

Molière, <u>Theatre complet illustre, Don Juan ou</u> <u>le festin de pierre</u>, Paris, Editorial Larousse.

Nietzsche, Friedrich, <u>The Birth of Tragedy</u> and <u>The Geneology of Morals</u>, Doubleday Anchor, 1956.

Ortega y Gasset, José, <u>Obras completas</u>, Madrid, 1938.

Peers, Allison E., <u>A History of the Romantic</u> <u>Movement in Spain</u>, Hafner Publishing Co., 1964, Vols. I and II.

<u>Angel de Saavedra, Duque</u> <u>de Rivas</u>, in Revue Hispanique, Número 133, 1923, Vol. 58.

Peyre, Henri, <u>Les générations litteraires</u>, París, Editorial Boivin, 1948.

Pineyro, Enrique, <u>The Romantics of Spain</u>, Institute of Hispanic Studies, 1934.

Praz, Mario, <u>La carne, la morte e il diávolo</u> <u>nella letterature romantica</u>, Firenze, Sansoni, Editore, 1948.

Rivera, Juan Ayuso, El concepto de la muerte en la poesía romántica Española, Madrid, Fundación Universitaria Española, 1959.

Reed, Albert Granberry, The Romantic Period, U.S.A., Scribner's Sons, 1929.

Richardson, Samuel, Clarrisa, or the History of a Young Lady, New York, Dutton, 1965.

Roaten, Parnell H., and F. Sánchez y Escribano, Wölfflin's Principles in Spanish Drama 1500-1700, Hispanic Institute in the United States, New York, 1952.

Saavedra, Angel de, Don Alvaro o la fuerza del sino in El teatro Español of Federico Carlos Sainz de Robles, Tomo VI, M. Aguilar, 1943.

Sypher, Wylie, Rococo to Cubism in Art and Literature, New York, Vintage, 1963.

Sade, The Marquis de, The Complete Justine, Philosophy in the Bedroom, and other writings, New York, Grove Press, Inc., 1966.

Sainz de Robles, Federico Carlos, El teatro Español, Madrid, Aguilar, 1943.

Staël, Madame de, On Politics, Literature, and National Character, New York, Doubleday and Co., Inc., 1965.

Tirso de Molina, El vergonzoso en palacio y El burlador de Sevilla, 2, Clásicos Castellanos, Madrid, Espasa-Calpe, S.A., 1958.

Valbuena Prat, Angel, Historia del teatro Español, Barcelona, Editorial Noguer, S.A., 1956.

Van Tieghem, Paul, El romanticismo en la literatura europea, México Unión Tipografía Editorial Hispana-América, 1958.

Walzel, Oskar, <u>German Romanticism</u>, New York, Capricorn, 1966.

Wellek, Rene, <u>Concepts of Criticism</u>, New Haven, Yale University Press, 1967.

Weinstein, Leo, <u>The Metamorphoses of Don Juan</u>, New York AMS Press, Inc., 1967.

Zorrilla, José, <u>Don Juan Tenorio</u>, y <u>El puñal del Godo</u>, 180, Madrid, Espasa-Calpe, S.A., 1965.

<u>Tres piezas teatrales</u>, Madrid, Aguilar, 1957.

ABOUT THE AUTHOR

John Reyna Tapia was born in Ajo, Arizona. He is a veteran of WW II, Korea, Vietnam Era, and is the recipient of seven Purple Hearts. Duties in the military included Chief U.S. Army Advisor to the Chilean Armed Forces; Operations Officer, School of the Americas, Canal Zone; Assistant Professor, Military Science; Advisor to U.S. Army Reserve Units. He also served as a Parachutist.

He is presently Chairman, Department of Foreign Languages at Fort Lewis College, Durango, Colorado. He has taught Spanish at the University of Utah, Western Michigan University, and Southern Illinois University. His degrees include the BA, LLB, MA, JD, and PhD. A member of many scholarly societies, he is the Colorado State Director for Sigma Delta Pi, National Spanish Honor Society. He is a Fellow of the International Academy of Poets, and has been recognized in a number of biographical publications including "Who's Who in Hispanic Letters in the United States." He is the poetry editor for the Durango Herald newspaper.